Essentials
of CAS Assessment

Essentials of Psychological Assessment Series

Series Editors, Alan S. Kaufman and Nadeen L. Kaufman

Essentials of WAIS-III Assessment
by Alan S. Kaufman and Elizabeth O. Lichtenberger

Essentials of Millon Inventories Assessment
by Stephen N. Strack

Essentials of NEPSY Assessment
by Sally Kemp, Ursula Kirk, and Marit Korkman

Essentials of Forensic Assessment
by Marc J. Ackerman

Essentials of Bayley Scales of Infant Development II Assessment
by Maureen M. Black and Kathleen Matula

Essentials of MMPI-2 Assessment
by David S. Nichol

Essentials

of CAS Assessment

Jack A. Naglieri

John Wiley & Sons, Inc.

NEW YORK • CHICHESTER • WEINHEIM • BRISBANE • SINGAPORE • TORONTO

This publication is designed to provide accurate and authoritative information in regard to the subject matter covered. It is sold with the understanding that the publisher is not engaged in rendering professional services. If legal, accounting, medical, psychological or any other expert assistance is required, the services of a competent professional person should be sought.

Library of Congress Cataloging-in-Publication Data:

Naglieri, Jack A.
    Essentials of CAS assessment / Jack A. Naglieri.
      p. cm. — (Essentials of psychological assessment series)
    Includes bibliographical references and index.
    ISBN 0-471-29015-7 (pbk : alk. paper)
    1. Das–Naglieri Cognitive Assessment System. I. Title.
  II. Title: Essentials of cognitive assessment system assessment. III. Series.
  BF432.5.D37N34 1999
  155.4'139323—dc21
                                       98-40739
                                          CIP

Printed in the United States of America.

10 9 8 7 6 5 4 3

This book is dedicated to my family, Diane, Andrea, Antonia, and Jack Jr., whose love is the driving force behind my work.

CONTENTS

ACKNOWLEDGMENTS

During the course of our professional careers there are often key people who influence us in significant ways. From the time I was a Ph.D. student at the University of Georgia until today Alan S. Kaufman has been that type of person for me. He helped me discover the world of test development and helped give me the tools I needed to succeed. Most importantly, he helped me see that the practice of intelligence testing could be changed if we provided instruments that encouraged the evolution of the field. I acknowledge and thank both Alan and Nadeen Kaufman for their suggestion that I write this book and their support and friendship over the last twenty years.

SERIES PREFACE

In the *Essentials of Psychological Assessment* series, we have attempted to provide the reader with books that will deliver key practical information in the most efficient and accessible style. The series features instruments in a variety of domains, such as cognition, personality, education, and neuropsychology. For the experienced clinician, books in the series will offer a concise yet thorough way to master utilization of the continuously evolving supply of new and revised instruments as well as a convenient method for keeping up to date on the tried-and-true measures. The novice will find here a prioritized assembly of all the information and techniques that must be at one's fingertips to begin the complicated process of individual psychological diagnosis.

Wherever feasible, visual shortcuts to highlight key points are utilized alongside systematic, step-by-step guidelines. Chapters are focused and succinct. Topics are targeted for an easy understanding of the essentials of administration, scoring, interpretation, and clinical application. Theory and research are continually woven into the fabric of each book, but always to enhance clinical inference, never to sidetrack or overwhelm. We have long been advocates of "intelligent" testing—the notion that a profile of test scores is meaningless unless it is brought to life by the clinical observations and astute detective work of knowledgeable examiners. Test profiles must be used to make a difference in the child's or adult's life, or why bother to test? We want this series to help our readers become the best intelligent testers they can be.

In *Essentials of CAS Assessment*, Dr. Jack Naglieri introduces an exciting new theory-based test, the Cognitive Assessment System (CAS). As coauthor of the CAS and frequent lecturer on its application and use, Dr. Naglieri offers readers an authoritative and insightful look at this new alternative for the cognitive assessment of children and adolescents. His enthusiasm for his new test and the Luria-based theory that forms its foundation is augmented by a growing body of data-based research that provides the core of his straightforward interpretive approach.

Alan S. Kaufman, Ph.D., and Nadeen L. Kaufman, Ed.D., Series Editors
Yale University School of Medicine

Essentials
of CAS Assessment

One

OVERVIEW

INTRODUCTION

Technology is the key to the future in any profession, and psychology is no exception. Psychologists who know the strengths and weaknesses of psychological technology have a clear advantage over those who do not. Those who keep pace with changing technology are better informed and, therefore, more able to make good decisions regarding children and their educational performance. The purpose of this book is to encourage a technological step in the field of intelligence testing.

The technology discussed in this book reflects important changes that have been occurring in psychology over the past 40 years. Many psychologists have suggested that the basic building blocks of intelligence should be identified and measured in an IQ test. This book, which features the Das-Naglieri Cognitive Assessment System, or CAS (Naglieri & Das, 1997a), provides information about such an approach. In addition to key findings from researchers and scholars who study the theoretical aspects of intelligence, the approach includes important concepts from applied psychology. Thus a strong theoretical perspective is provided, and practical ways to apply the theory are included. Real-life case studies as well as research reports illustrate how theory can be applied.

Essentials of CAS Assessment is designed to give professionals a way to quickly obtain knowledge of new intelligence testing technology—the Das-Naglieri CAS, or CAS as it is referred to in this book. In an easy-to-read format, this book covers a history of IQ testing; strengths and weaknesses of traditional testing technology; the Planning, Attention, Simultaneous, and Successive (PASS) theory, and the test itself, as alternatives to traditional approaches; administration, scoring, and interpretation; and extension of results for intervention purposes. The ultimate goal is to describe both the CAS and the PASS theory on which CAS is based to enable readers to utilize this instrument within the context of the theory. Emphasis is given to the importance of the PASS theory and practical application of the CAS for (a) effective evaluation of children's cognitive performance, and (b) consideration of this information for diagnosis and intervention.

HISTORY OF IQ AND DEVELOPMENT OF NEW TECHNOLOGY

Before discussing the history and development of the CAS, it is appropriate to reflect on the history of the intelligence tests used today, especially the Wechsler and Binet scales. These tests have defined the construct of intelligence ever since they were developed in the early part of the 20th century, because they have provided structured and useful methods by which to evaluate children and adults. The Wechsler and Binet tests have been applied in virtually all areas of psychology, but especially in clinical, developmental, educational, and industrial areas. They have been used for so long because research has shown that IQ is significantly correlated with achievement, related to acquisition of knowledge in employment settings, related to acquisition of knowledge in nonacademic settings, and even related to acquisition of knowledge by one's children (Brody,

≣Rapid Reference

90 Years of Stanford-Binet Scales

- 1905 First Binet scale is published by Binet and Simon, subsequently revised in 1908
- 1909 Goddard translates Binet-Simon from French to English
- 1916 Terman publishes the Stanford Revision and Extension of the Binet-Simon scales that is normed on American children and adolescents and becomes widely used
- 1937 Terman and Merrill publish a revision of the 1916 scale called the Stanford-Binet Intelligence Scale
- 1960 Stanford-Binet, Form LM (Second Edition)
- 1972 Stanford-Binet, Form LM (Third Edition)
- 1986 Stanford-Binet Fourth Edition (by Thorndike, Hagen, & Sattler, 1986)

1992). Because of these factors and the practical utility of IQ tests, these general measures of intelligence have enjoyed widespread use for nearly 100 years (see Rapid References on pages 2–4).

Although the Wechsler and Binet tests are widely used and the most well known measures of intelligence, they have one essential limitation—they represent a technology that has not changed since Binet and Simon introduced their first scale in 1905 and Wechsler published his first test in 1939. The Fourth Edition of the Stanford-Binet and the latest revisions of the Wechsler scales (e.g., Wechsler Adult Intelligence Scale—Third Edition; Wechsler, 1997) are essentially the same as their respective early versions despite cosmetic modifications and improved standardization samples. Some psychologists have noted this stagnation. For example, Cronbach (1970) stated that "tests in general use today are much like those of the 1920s. Current tests differ from those of the earlier generation just as the 1970 automobiles differ from those of 1920: more efficient, more elegant, but operating on the same principles as before" (p. 199). Of course, Cronbach's "today" is nearly 30 years earlier from the day this book was written! But why are the tests so similar, and why have they remained the same for so long?

Intelligence test content became solidified at the early stages of IQ test development, mainly because of the profound impact of the work of Alfred Binet. This influence was noted by Yoakum and Yerkes (1920), who stated that the "origin of general intelligence tests is due to the genius of Alfred Binet" (p. 1). Following Binet and Simon's 30-item scale published in 1905 (see Rapid Reference on page 5), they further refined their tests, as did psychologists in the United States, resulting in several versions of the Binet-Simon scale—for example, the Goddard, Kuhlmann, and Stanford revisions

≡ Rapid Reference

60 Years of Wechsler Scales

- 1939 Wechsler-Bellevue, Form I
- 1946 Wechsler-Bellevue, Form II
- 1949 Wechsler Intelligence Scale for Children (WISC)
- 1955 Wechsler Adult Intelligence Scale (WAIS)
- 1967 Wechsler Preschool and Primary Scale of Intelligence (WPPSI)
- 1974 WISC—Revised
- 1981 WAIS—Revised
- 1989 WPPSI—Revised
- 1991 WISC-III
- 1997 WAIS-III

of the Binet. Those who developed the Army mental testing program also relied heavily on the work of Binet for the examination of a large number of adults entering military service during World War I (Yoakum & Yerkes, 1920). At that time there was considerable borrowing of methods and tests, which is well documented in the various sources that report on development of the first intelligence tests (e.g., see Pintner, 1923). The extensive "borrowing from a common professional or scientific pool" (Matarazzo, 1972, p. 44) resulted in the similarity of IQ tests for both individual and group testing purposes.

Perhaps the most important utilization of a common professional or scientific pool of techniques for individual IQ tests occurred when David Wechsler adapted the group and individual tests utilized by the Army into a single measure, which became the Wechsler-Bellevue Intelligence Scale (Wechsler, 1939). The hallmark of Wechsler's contribution was his ability to transform the group and individual testing procedures of the Army mental testing program, and the work of Binet, into an individually administered test that clinical psychologists could use to evaluate adults. Wechsler incorporated tests such as the Manikin and Feature Profile (now Object Assembly), the Maze Test (now Mazes), the Digit Symbol Test (now Digit Symbol), Picture Arrangement (now by the same name), Picture Completion (now by the same name), and Cube Construction (a variant is now Block Design), as well as tests currently named Arithmetic, Comprehension, Similarities, and Information. The original versions of these tests are amply illustrated in Yoakum and Yerkes's (1920) book (see pp. 102–124, 205–275). These tests were incorporated into the various versions of the Wechsler scales (the preschool, child, and adult scales) and are apparent in the most recent edition, the Wechsler Adult Intelligence Scale—Third Edition (WAIS-III; Wechsler, 1997). Because the scales have remained essentially the same since 1939, and because of the similarity of the Wechsler

Rapid Reference

Who Initiated the Term *Test*?

According to Pintner (1923) we are indebted to J. McK. Cattell for using the word *test* "as denoting a simple task to be performed by subjects in the investigation of individual differences" (p. 15). In addition, in 1890 Cattell called for "standardization of methods of procedure, and [urged] the necessity for the establishment of norms" (p. 15).

≡ *Rapid Reference*

The 1905 version of the Binet included 30 subtests (Pintner, 1923, p. 94), some of which are identified here:

1. Ability to follow movement of a lighted match with the eyes
2. Ability to grasp a piece of wood with the hand
3. Recognition of food
4. Execution of simple commands and imitation of gestures
5. Naming of parts of the body, familiar objects, and pictures of things
6. Comparison of the length of two lines and comparison of two weights
7. Repetition of sentences and digits
8. Comparison of the differences between objects (e.g., a fly and a butterfly)
9. Memory for pictures of common objects
10. Completion of incomplete sentences
11. Paper cutting
12. Definition of abstract terms

scales to the tests used by the Army during World War I and to the Stanford-Binet, there have been both uniformity and continuity of IQ test content throughout the 20th century.

Since the initial formulation of the Binet and Wechsler scales, there has been a consolidation of thinking that intelligence *is* what these tests measure. Their similarity of content, and the way each is used to demonstrate the validity of the other, reinforce the view that intelligence is best measured by the tests that have been in existence for about 100 years. That is not to say that there has been a marked change in the things any practical test of intelligence should be capable of (see Rapid Reference on page 6), but there has been considerable evolution in researchers' and practitioners' understanding of intelligence, especially as it relates to specific cognitive abilities.

It is important to consider, however, that the fact that IQ tests have remained stable during the 20th century does not contradict the evidence that the tests can be effective. As noted previously, despite the criticism of intelligence tests, they have been shown to be effective as measures of general intelligence. Where IQ tests fail is in situations when more information than the

≡ Rapid Reference

Army Mental Testing Program

The test should ...

1. be suitable for group administration.
2. have high validity as a measure of intelligence.
3. have sufficient ceiling and floor.
4. be objective to score.
5. be scored rapidly with the least chance of error.
6. have two forms of equal difficulty to prevent coaching.
7. include a method to detect malingering.
8. be constructed to reduce cheating.
9. be independent of schooling and educational advantages.
10. require a minimum of written answers.
11. be of interest to the subjects.
12. yield an accurate measure in a short time.

Note. From Yoakum & Yerkes (1920, p. 3).

general IQ score is needed. Interestingly, the limit of the global IQ to predict success was noted by Wechsler when he was assigned to the psychology unit at Fort Logan, Texas, during World War I. According to Matarazzo (1972), Wechsler used the Stanford-Binet, Yerkes Point Scale, and Army Individual Performance scales to "evaluate the military fitness of recruits who repeatedly failed on standardized tests, but who nevertheless gave histories of adequate work performance and adjustment in civilian life" (p. 73). This experience led Wechsler to consider non-intellectual factors to explain the test's failure. Another view is that then, like now, the general intelligence approach failed to account for variation because it did not provide essential information about specific abilities. In today's context, the content of the general intelligence

DON'T FORGET

Psychology has advanced considerably during the 20th century, especially in the knowledge of specific abilities and the essential cognitive processes that make up intelligence.

test does not allow for sensitivity to the specific cognitive problems that underlie, for example, learning disabilities and attention deficits. What is needed is a more finely refined measure of the basic building blocks of intelligence—that is, a theory that includes specific cognitive abilities.

Groundwork for Change

During the 20th century, but especially during the latter half, considerable research has been conducted on the construct of intelligence. In particular there has been much ex-

> ### DON'T FORGET
>
> The **concept of general intelligence** was assumed to exist, and psychologists went about "the measurement of an individual's general ability without waiting for an adequate psychological definition" (Pintner, 1923, p. 52). Moreover, "psychologists borrowed from every-day life a vague term implying all-round ability and knowledge, and in the process of trying to measure this trait he [Binet] has been and still is attempting to define it more sharply and endow it with a stricter scientific connotation" (Pintner, 1923, p. 53).

amination of specific abilities that extend beyond the concept of general, undifferentiated intelligence. These efforts address the concerns of early IQ test developers who thought it was not possible to measure aspects of intelligence and that only general (complex) capacity without the contribution of each to the total could be assessed (Cronbach, 1970). But in the 1960s, in particular, a growing number of cognitive theorists studied neuropsychology, neuroscience, and higher mental processes. Described as the cognitive revolution (Miller, Galanter, & Pribram, 1960), this movement had a substantial influence in theoretical psychology and more recently in applied psychology. The impact of the cognitive revolution was first felt with the publication of the Kaufman Assessment Battery for Children (Kaufman & Kaufman, 1983) and most recently with the publication of the CAS in 1997. Although the knowledge generated by these cognitive researchers, like the work of other psychologists, provided the opportunity to influence the practice of traditional intelligence testing, IQ testing nevertheless remained firmly rooted in the Wechsler and Binet approaches. In fact, the stagnation of intelligence tests is apparent in Brody's (1992) statement: "I do not believe that our intellectual progress has had a major impact on the development of tests of intelligence" (p. 355).

CAUTION

When is a new test really new?

It is easy to think that newly published and recently revised tests are new, but in fact they may be old ideas presented in a new package.

Technology Determines What Is Measured

The technology used in any scientific field has a profound impact because it determines the content and scope of the information obtained. The technology therefore determines what is possible. There have been significant advances during the 20th century in other branches of science that were made possible by the technology that was used. For example, from 1907 to 1969 aviation technology moved from the Wright brothers' "Flyer" to the *Apollo 11* mission that brought Neil Armstrong to the lunar surface. The latter event was even more profound because viewers around the world actually watched the first step on the moon as it happened—something that was unimaginable in the Wright brothers' time. Armstrong's famous statement, "One small step for man, one giant leap for mankind," spoke to the power of modern technology. In medicine, the technology of today allows for organ transplants—something that was surely viewed as science fiction for the young Alfred Binet, M.D. Astronomers of today use modern technology like the spectroscope, radio wave telescope, and Hubble telescope to see new galaxies that were inaccessible with the technology of the early 20th century. Indeed, technology can enlighten or limit us because it determines what we know.

DON'T FORGET

The technology one uses determines what information is obtained. Therefore, the validity of the technology has a profound impact on professional practice. As technology changes, so does the information obtained and the effectiveness of the professional who uses it.

The Changing Face of IQ Testing

Traditional IQ technology, crystallized by the seminal work of Binet and Wechsler as well as others, has played a critical and profound role in psychology, making intelligence testing among the most important contributions psychology has made to society (Anastasi & Urbina, 1997). But this technology has limits; because it is locked in time—circa 1900—it has not had the advantage of our increased understanding of specific human abilities.

There has been a significant movement toward measuring specific abilities as alternatives to traditional IQ tests (Naglieri, 1997a). This new breed of tests includes the CAS (Naglieri & Das, 1997a), Differential Ability Scales (DAS; Elliott, 1990), Kaufman Adolescent and Adult Intelligence Test (KAIT;

> **CAUTION**
> ....
> **Does old mean bad?**
> Traditional IQ tests have withstood the test of time and are in widespread use today because they are effective. Their limitation is that they do not measure specific abilities that modern psychology has identified since the early part of the 20th century. In addition, because traditional IQ tests don't measure specific abilities, they have limited utility for detecting specific problems children have that can lead to academic failure.

Kaufman & Kaufman, 1993), K-ABC (Kaufman & Kaufman, 1983), and Woodcock-Johnson Revised Tests of Cognitive Ability (WJ-R; Woodcock & Johnson, 1989b). The authors of these tests have all made efforts to modernize the traditional IQ test technology that has dominated most of the 20th century. In fact, the single most important goal of the Cognitive Assessment System is to encourage an evolutionary step from the traditional IQ, general ability approach to a theory-based, multidimensional view with constructs built on contemporary research in human cognition.

THEORETICAL FOUNDATION OF CAS

The PASS (Planning, Attention, Simultaneous, and Successive) theory is based on the neuropsychological, information processing, and cognitive psychological research of A. R. Luria (1966, 1973, 1980, 1982). According to Solso and Hoffman (1991), Luria is the "most frequently cited Soviet scholar in American, British, and Canadian psychology periodicals" (p. 251).

Roots of PASS

Luria's view of the basic cognitive processes was partially based on his own research and the integration of his findings with those of other researchers. He gives ample credit to those from whose work he drew information about the specific functions of the brain in his book, *The Working Brain: An Introduction to Neuropsychology* (1966). Luria described the basic building blocks of intelligence as functional systems, meaning that there are basic cognitive processes that provide the "ability" to perform certain acts, each of which is distinctive in character. These basic cognitive processes, or functions, were associated with different areas of the brain by a number of researchers whom Luria (1966) amply recognized.

Luria associated each of the functional units with specific regions of the brain. The first functional unit is associated with the brain stem, diencephalon, and medial regions of the hemispheres. The occipital, parietal, and temporal lobes posterior to the central sulcus regulate the second unit's functions. The third functional unit's functions are regulated by the frontal lobes, especially the prefrontal region. These functional units, illustrated in Figure 1.1, are described in the following section.

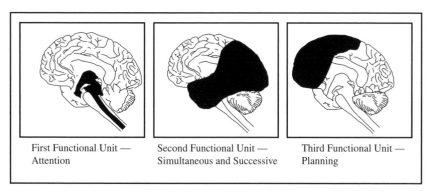

First Functional Unit —
Attention

Second Functional Unit —
Simultaneous and Successive

Third Functional Unit —
Planning

Figure 1.1   Three Functional Units and Associated Brain Structures

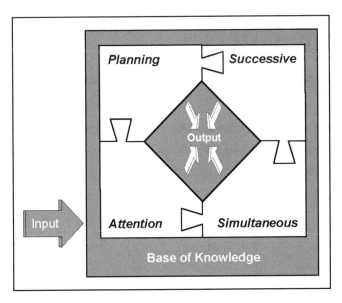

Figure 1.2 PASS Theory Diagram

PASS Theory

The PASS theory provides a view of intelligence that is considerably different from the general ability approach. The theory proposes that Planning, Attention, Simultaneous, and Successive cognitive processes are the basic building blocks of human intellectual functioning. These four processes are interrelated and interact with an individual's base of knowledge, as shown in Figure 1.2. According to this theory, human cognitive functioning includes four components:

Planning processes provide cognitive control, utilization of processes and knowledge, intentionality, and self-regulation to achieve a desired goal;

Attentional processes provide focused, selective cognitive activity and resistance to distraction; and

Simultaneous and *Successive* processes are the two forms of operating on information.

Luria's three functional units include the four PASS processes as follows: Attention is in the first functional unit, Simultaneous and Successive are in the second, and Planning is in the third. The subsequent discussion illustrates each process; one subtest from each of the four scales of the CAS is shown, and examples of children's classwork that involve the process are illustrated. The discussion is organized according to the PASS theory, beginning with Planning, then covering Attention, and concluding with Simultaneous and Successive processes.

Planning

According to Naglieri and Das (1997c), "planning is a mental process by which the individual determines, selects, applies, and evaluates solutions to problems" (p. 2). The process provides the means to solve problems of varying complexity and

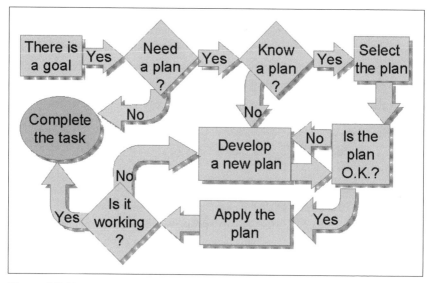

Figure 1.3 Structural Architecture of Planning Processing

may involve attentional, simultaneous, and successive processes as well as knowledge. Success on CAS Planning subtests requires the child to develop a plan of action, evaluate the value of the method, monitor its effectiveness, revise or reject a previous plan as the task demands change, and control the impulse to act without careful consideration (see Figure 1.3). Planning is central to all activities in which there are both intentionality and a need for some method to solve a problem. This process includes self-monitoring and impulse control as well as plan generation. All the CAS Planning subtests require

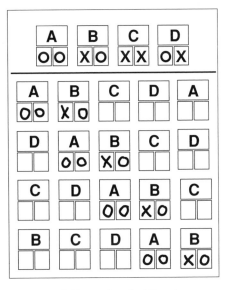

Figure 1.4 Example of a Planning Test Item

the use of strategies for efficient performance and the application of these strategies to novel tasks of relatively reduced complexity. The use of strategies to solve Planning tests is amply documented in Naglieri and Das (1997c).

Planning as a process that demands the development and use of strategies to solve problems is well illustrated by the Planned Codes test on the CAS (see Figure 1.4). This test requires the child to write a code (e.g., OO or XO) under the corresponding letter (e.g., A or B). Children can use different strategies to complete the test in an efficient and timely manner. For example, a large percentage of children use a strategy that involves completing the page by letter, which is associated with high scores on the Planning subtest (Naglieri & Das, 1997c). The child who develops and utilizes a plan, and does so with careful monitoring of the demands of the task, earns a high score. In contrast, children who do not use strategies earn lower scores (see Naglieri & Das, 1997c, pp. 86, 88). The important point is that this test is sensitive to planning because the scores reflect *how* the child meets the demands of the task. How one decides to do things involves planning processes.

Planning processes are involved in many tasks children complete in school. One activity is illustrated in Figure 1.5 for learning to spell. The focus

Spelling Study Guide

Name _____

This week's words

1. _____
2. _____
3. _____
4. _____
5. _____
6. _____
7. _____
8. _____
9. _____
10. _____
11. _____
12. _____
13. _____
14. _____
15. _____

Don't let Friday's test sneak up on you. Follow these study tips this week.

• Don't wait until the last minute.

• Study 10 to 15 minutes each day.

• Post the list on your refrigerator.

• Take advantage of extra minutes to study.

• Study with a friend or family member.

Choose a study activity to do each night. Write the day in the appropriate blank.

_____ Use flashcards.

_____ Study with a friend.

_____ Write the words 10 times.

_____ Write each word in a sentence.

_____ Use a tape recorder.

_____ Make a word search puzzle.

Figure 1.5 Illustration of a Worksheet That Involves Planning

of this worksheet is to encourage children to consider *how* to learn the words. It does not simply tell them what words to learn, but rather suggests different ways to learn to spell and try various methods. It is expected that this approach will also encourage children to figure out which method allows them to acquire the words best. This activity facilitates and encourages a planful approach to learning and at the same time encourages the children to learn to spell specific words for the week.

Attention

Naglieri and Das (1997c) describe Attention as "a mental process by which the individual selectively focuses on particular stimuli while inhibiting responses to competing stimuli presented over time" (p. 3). Attentional processes are assessed by CAS tasks that demand focused, selective, sustained, and effortful activity. *Focused attention* involves directed concentration toward a particular activity, but *selective attention* requires the inhibition of responses to distracting stimuli. *Sustained attention* refers to the variation of performance over time, which can be influenced by the different amount of effort required to solve the test. All CAS Attention subtests present children with competing demands on their attention and require sustained focus, as illustrated in Figure 1.6.

Attention processes are well illustrated by the CAS subtest Number Detection. Figure 1.7 provides an item like those included in this subtest. In this example the child must underline all the numbers 1, 2, 4, and 5 on that page, but only when they are printed in the correct font. Each stimulus (the number) has two dimensions, the number and the font. The child may find, for example, the number 1; but unless it is printed in the correct font, it is not a target (a number that should be underlined). Thus the test presents the child with stimuli that have two dimensions—a number and a font, or the way the number is printed—and the child responds to (underlines) or does not respond to (ignores) each number according

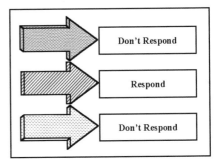

Figure 1.6 Structural Architecture of Attentional Processing

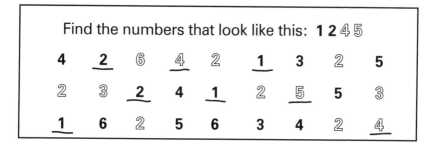

Figure 1.7 Example of an Attention Test Item

to its characteristics. This response environment places strong demands on Attention.

An example of a school activity that has strong attentional demands is provided in Figure 1.8. This math worksheet involves all the PASS processes, but especially Attention because of the structure of the questions. For example, in the first question ("What is the number for 1 ten 5 ones?") the child has several distracting options. The 1 can be in any location, but is that location the 10s place? This creates an environment with targets (the 10s place) and distractors (the ones or 100s place). The "respond" (i.e., choose this location) or "do not respond" (i.e., put a 1 in the ones place) environment demands selective attention and resistance to distraction. This particular worksheet is made even more complex by the requirement to find two numbers, each of which could appear in any location.

When examining children's

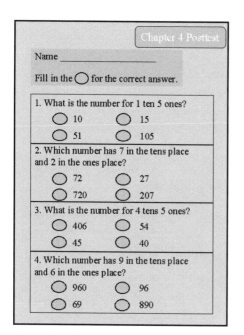

Figure 1.8 Illustration of a Worksheet That Involves Attention

worksheets like this one for Attention, it is important to remember that all PASS processes are involved in most things people do. For example, Successive processing is needed for determining the sequence of ones, 10s, and 100s place; and Planning is needed for organizing how the task will be completed and for exerting impulse control. But the key to this task (assuming the child knows the difference between 10s and ones place) is that it has a heavy demand on (is weighted toward) Attention.

Simultaneous Processing

"Simultaneous processing is a mental process by which the individual integrates separate stimuli into a single whole or group (Luria, 1970)" (Naglieri & Das, 1997c, p. 4). The essential ingredient of Simultaneous processing is that the person must see how all the separate elements are interrelated in a conceptual whole (see Figure 1.9). Simultaneous processing has strong spatial and logical dimensions for both nonverbal and verbal (e.g., grammar) content. The spatial aspect of Simultaneous processing includes perception of stimuli as a whole. Simultaneous processing is involved in understanding grammatical statements that demand the integration of words into a whole idea. This integration involves comprehension of word relationships, prepositions, and inflections so the person can obtain meaning based on the whole idea. Simultaneous processing subtests included in CAS require integration of parts into a single whole and understanding of logical and grammatical relationships. These processes are used in tests that involve nonverbal and verbal content, as well as recall of the stimuli, but the essential ingredient is Simultaneous processing.

Figure 1.10 provides an example of an item like those found in the CAS Verbal-Spatial Relations subtest. In this item the child must decide which of the six options shows "the arrow pointing to the square in the circle." In order to solve this problem, the child must understand the relationships among each of the objects (in this case

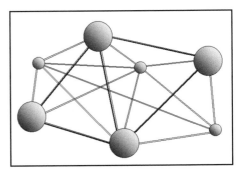

Figure 1.9 Structural Architecture of Simultaneous Processing

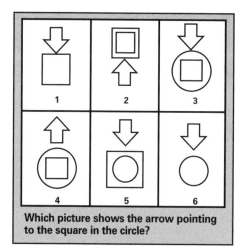

Which picture shows the arrow pointing to the square in the circle?

Figure 1.10 Example of a Simultaneous Processing Test Item

an arrow, circle, and square) to determine which option matches the written statement. This test item demands Simultaneous processing because the child must organize the three objects into a whole to solve the problem.

An example of a child's school activity that has strong demands on Simultaneous processing is provided in Figure 1.11. In this worksheet the child is asked to draw a diagram from four perspectives. Thus the child has to understand the relationships among each of the blocks when viewed from different perspectives. Then the child must produce a drawing in two dimensions that shows how the blocks would look from each perspective. The strong spatial dimension to the task is obvious. How might Planning become important? If the child decided to build each diagram using real blocks and then view that production from each perspective.

Successive Processing

Naglieri and Das (1997c) describe Successive processing as "a mental process by which the individual integrates stimuli into a specific serial order that forms a chain-like progression" (p. 5), as shown in Figure 1.12. Successive processing is required when a person must arrange things "in a strictly defined order" (Luria, 1966, p. 78). The distinguishing quality of a task that demands Successive processing is that each element is only related to those that precede it, and these stimuli are not interrelated. Successive processing involves both the perception of stimuli in sequence and the formation of sounds and movements in order. For this reason, Successive processing has strong sequential components and is involved with the syntax of language.

The serial organization of spoken speech and the production of "separate sounds and motor impulses into consecutive series" (Luria & Tsvetkova, 1990, p. xvi) are tasks that involve Successive processing. It allows for the

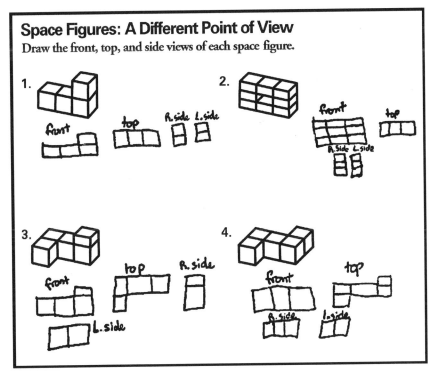

Figure 1.11   Illustration of a Worksheet That Involves Simultaneous Processing

comprehension of the meaning of speech when the "individual elements of the whole narrative always behave as if organized in certain successive series" (Luria, 1966, p. 78) because the serial presentation of the narrative determines the meaning. Successive processing subtests included in CAS require the reproduction of the serial dimension of stimuli through understanding of

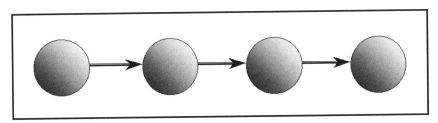

Figure 1.12   Structural Architecture of Successive Processing

1. The blue is yellow. Who is yellow?

2. The red greened the blue with a yellow. Who used the yellow?

3. The red blues a yellow green of pinks, that are brown in the purple, and then grays the tan. What does the red do first?

Figure 1.13 Example of a Successive Processing Test Item

sentences on the basis of syntactic relationships, and the articulation of words in series or the repetition of words or a series of words in series.

A test that involves Successive processing must demand that the child attend to and work with the linear order of events. This is most easily evaluated by the CAS subtest Word Series. In this subtest the child simply repeats words in the exact order in which they are stated by the examiner. A more complex successive CAS subtest is Sentence Questions. This subtest, illustrated in Figure 1.13, requires the child to answer a question about a statement made by the examiner. For example, the examiner says, "The red greened the blue with a yellow. Who used the yellow?" and the child should say "the red." This item requires that the child comprehend the sequence of words to arrive at the correct solution, making it an excellent measure of Successive processing.

Like the previously discussed PASS processes, Successive processing is involved in children's schoolwork. For example, when a child is asked to round a number, he or she may follow prescribed steps to complete the task. A 10-year-old girl used the following steps to round the number .386 to the nearest 100ths.

1. "If you look at the 100s place, an 8 is there;
2. then you look at the number next to it [she points to the number 6] and see a 6.
3. A 6 is higher than 5 so you turn the 8 to a 9.
4. Everything in front of it [she points to the number 3] stays the same.
5. So the answer is .39."

In this example there is a carefully executed series of events, and these steps are used to accomplish the task.

The emphasis on the steps or successive series of events is also involved in reading, especially in initial reading or decoding of unfamiliar words. In the example shown in Figure 1.14, the child is presented with easily confusable words and must focus carefully on the pronunciation of sounds in order. In addition, the child must learn the association of the sounds, in order, with the letters of the words—which demands Successive processing. This point will be discussed in Chapter 6 when reading-disabled children's performance in Successive processing on CAS is examined.

Relationships Among the PASS Processes

The four PASS processes are not unrelated abilities that function in isolation. In fact, the opposite is as-

Figure 1.14 Illustration of a Worksheet That Involves Successive Processing of Sounds in Order

sumed. As stated by Luria (1973), "each form of conscious activity is always a *complex functional system* and takes place through *the combined working of all three brain units*, each of which makes its own contribution. The well established fact of modern psychology provides a solid basis for this view" (p. 99). [Emphasis in original.] This conception means that the four PASS processes are interdependently involved in activity and interact with the person's fund of knowledge.

For example, the child, in the early stages of reading, might use Planning processes when making decisions about what to read, finding the first page, and determining how to decode each word. Attention is needed to focus on the appropriate stimuli and ignore distractions. Simultaneous processing is involved in seeing the sentence as a whole, and Successive processing is used to decode words and comprehend information on the basis of syntax or ordering of events. All PASS processes are involved, but at any point there may be a shift in the contribution each is making to the particular goal. For example,

DON'T FORGET

All PASS processes are involved in most things people do. Sometimes one or two of the PASS processes dominate an activity. Sometimes one process is critical to successful completion. CAS subtests have been carefully developed so that they are consistently influenced by one of the four processes. In contrast, schoolwork often involves many of the PASS processes. When examining children's work, look for how each of the processes is involved and determine which one or ones are especially important to success.

if an unknown word is found, the child may decide (use Planning) to decode the word phonetically (Successive), but if that does not work he or she may try to either see the word as a whole or group the letters (Simultaneous). During the procedure of reading, therefore, different processes may be relied on at different times to obtain meaning from the written words. Thus the PASS processes form functional systems, or a "working constellation" (Luria, 1966, p. 70), of cognitive activity, thereby permitting individuals to perform the same task with the contribution of various processes and the participation of the knowledge base. Effective functioning is accomplished through the integration of Planning, Attention, Simultaneous, and Successive processes (as well as the base of knowledge) as demanded by the particular task.

Although the PASS processes are interdependent, not every process is equally involved in every task. Tasks, like the CAS subtests, may be weighted, or heavily influenced by a single PASS process. For example, repetition of digits forward certainly involves Planning (the intention to do the task) and Attention, but the task is heavily weighted toward Successive processing. The parts of the item (digits) must be arranged in linear order for the response to be scored as correct; thus Successive processing has the most influence on the score. A second example, completion of progressive matrices, requires careful examination of the information provided (Planning and Attention). What is most important, however, is seeing the interrelationships among each of the diagrams in the matrix. This is why matrices are excellent measures of Simultaneous processing.

Because the emphasis is on the specific PASS process or processes involved with a task, the modality becomes less important. Information that is to be processed may arrive through any of the receptors (e.g., eyes, ears, skin, muscle movements) and be received in a serial (i.e., over time) or synchronous (i.e., concurrent) manner. That is, several stimuli may be presented to the individual at one time, or several stimuli may be presented one at a time (e.g., hearing two different words at the same time, or hearing two words in a series). Despite the type of presentation, the information is processed according to the requirements of the task and with the participation of all processes. For example, comprehension of an oral statement on the basis of syntax demands Successive processing (CAS Sentence Questions subtests), but comprehension of an oral statement that requires understanding of the grammatical structure of the sentence demands Simultaneous processing (CAS Verbal-Spatial Relations subtests).

COGNITIVE ASSESSMENT SYSTEM

The PASS theory was used as the basis for the CAS to provide an individually administered instrument for assessing cognitive functioning. The PASS theory guided the construction of the CAS, and the content of the test was not constrained by previous approaches to assessing intelligence. CAS developers incorporated the requirement of high psychometric qualities and a specific theory of cognitive processing within the context of providing a user-friendly, practical test. The CAS was developed to integrate both theoretical and applied knowledge in psychology.

Guidelines for Development of the CAS

There were several basic assumptions and goals when development of the CAS began:

1. A test of intelligence should be based on a theory of ability.
2. A theory of ability should be based on the view that intelligence is best described as cognitive processes, and the term *cognitive processes* should replace the term *intelligence*.

DON'T FORGET
....
The CAS is a new technology designed to merge theoretical advances regarding specific abilities with developments in psychometric methods made during the 20th century.

3. A theory of cognitive processes should (a) inform the user about those specific abilities that are related to academic and job successes and difficulties, (b) have relevance to differential diagnosis, and (c) provide guidance to the selection and/or development of effective programming for intervention.
4. A theory of cognitive functioning should be firmly based on a sizable research base and should have been proposed, tested, modified, and shown to have several kinds of validity.
5. A test of cognitive processing should follow closely from the theory of cognition on which it is based.
6. A test of cognitive processing should evaluate an individual through items that are as free from acquired knowledge as possible.

Using these concepts as a base, the CAS was developed to evaluate the four cognitive PASS processes (Planning, Attention, Simultaneous processing, and Successive processing) for individuals between the ages of 5 and 17. The PASS theory served as the base because, as Crocker and Algina (1986) point out, "psychological measurement, even though it is based on observable responses, . . . [has] little meaning or usefulness unless it could be interpreted in light of the underlying theoretical construct" (p. 7). The PASS theory defines the basic building blocks of intelligence.

Experimental Studies of PASS Leading to CAS

The development of tests to measure the PASS processes began with an examination by Das (1972) of the differences between persons with and without mental retardation. That study involved only Simultaneous and Successive cognitive processes but led to the suggestion that these two processes be included as a model for cognitive abilities (Das, Kirby, & Jarman, 1975). In their book *Simultaneous and Successive Cognitive Processes*, Das, Kirby, and Jarman (1979) presented tasks used to operationalize Simultaneous and Successive processes and discussed a need to develop measures of Attention and Planning.

Ashman and Das (1980) first reported the addition of Planning measures to Simultaneous and Successive experimental tasks. Attention and Planning tasks were developed and tested several years later and initially reported in the literature by Naglieri and Das (1987, 1988). Descriptions of the development and refinement of PASS experimental tests and efforts to evaluate their practical utility and validity are contained in more than 100 published papers and several books. See Kirby (1984) and Das, Naglieri, and Kirby (1994) for summaries of this research.

Development of CAS Subtests

CAS subtests were developed specifically to operationalize the Planning, Attention, Simultaneous, and Successive theory of cognitive processing. Selection of tests was not dictated or constrained by the inclusion of similar approaches in other theories of human cognitive abilities or tests of intelligence. The sole criterion for inclusion was each subtest's correspondence to the theoretical framework and functional demands of the PASS theory. Development of each CAS subtest was accomplished by following an experimental sequence involving item generation, data analysis, test revision, and reexamination until the instructions, items, and other dimensions were refined. Each subtest was evaluated through a series of pilot tests, research studies, a national tryout, and the national standardization. This process allowed the identification of subtests that were dominated by a particular process (rather than by tasks that demanded a particular process exclusively). Das, Kirby, and Jarman (1979) summarized the initial work involving Simultaneous and Successive processing; more recent findings are described by Das, Naglieri, and Kirby (1994) and Naglieri and Das (1997c).

Description of the Cognitive Assessment System

The CAS (see Rapid Reference on page 26) is organized according to the PASS theory and therefore comprises four scales. Each scale is made up of subtests that assess the corresponding process. In addition, a total Full Scale score is obtained from the sum of all the subtest scores.

Full Scale

The CAS yields an overall measure of cognitive functioning called the Full Scale (FS) score, which has a mean set at 100 and a standard deviation set at 15. The FS score is a standard score based on the equally weighted composite of scores on the Planning, Attention, Simultaneous, and Successive subtests.

≡ *Rapid Reference*

Cognitive Assessment System

Authors: Jack A. Naglieri, Ph.D. and J. P. Das, Ph.D.

Publication Date: 1997

What the Test Measures: PASS Theory of cognitive processing

Age Range: 5 years through 17 years 11 months

Administration Time: Basic Battery = 40 minutes; Standard Battery = 60 minutes

Qualification of Examiners: Graduate training in administration, scoring, and interpretation of individual intelligence tests

Publisher:

>Riverside Publishing Company
>425 Spring Lake Drive
>Itasca, IL 60143-2079

>Ordering phone number: 800-323-9540
>Fax: 630-467-7192
>Publisher: http://www.riverpub.com
>CAS: http://www.riverpub.com/products/clinical/cas.htm
>CAS complete test kit price = $578.00 (as of September 1998)

The FS score provides an index of the overall level of an individual's cognitive functioning. The Full Scale is considered a necessary, but potentially confusing, score that represents the combination of the PASS scales. Naglieri and Das (1997c) caution the user that if one or more of the PASS Scale standard scores shows significant variation (see Chapter 4 in this book), then the Full Scale score may "obscure important relative strengths and weaknesses" (p. 96) that may help explain the child's successes and failures. In such instances, overemphasis on the Full Scale score is to be especially avoided.

PASS Scales

The Planning, Attention, Simultaneous, and Successive scales are derived from the sum of subtests included in each respective scale. Like the Full Scale score, each PASS Scale has a normative mean of 100 and a standard deviation of 15. The PASS scales represent a child's cognitive functioning and are used

Table 1.1 Structure of the CAS Scales and Subtests

Full Scale

Planning

    * Matching Numbers (MN)

    * Planned Codes (PCd)

    Planned Connections (PCn)

Simultaneous

    * Nonverbal Matrices (NvM)

    * Verbal-Spatial Relations (VSR)

    Figure Memory (FM)

Attention

    * Expressive Attention (EA)

    * Number Detection (ND)

    Receptive Attention (RA)

Successive

    * Word Series (WS) and/or

    * Sentence Repetition (SR)

    Speech Rate (SpR, ages 5–7) or Sentence Questions (SQ, ages 8–17)

Note. Asterisk (*) indicates a subtest that is included in the Basic Battery.

in identification of specific strengths and weaknesses in cognitive processing. The PASS scales, not the PASS subtests, are the focus of CAS interpretation (see Chapter 4).

Subtests

Two combinations subtests are used to obtain PASS Scale and Full Scale scores. One is called the Basic Battery and the other the Standard Battery. The Basic Battery includes eight subtests (two per PASS Scale), and the Standard Battery includes all twelve subtests. The subtests and scales to which they are assigned are shown in Table 1.1 (an asterisk indicates subtests that are included in the

Basic Battery). Each subtest scaled score is set at a mean of 10 and a standard deviation of 3. The CAS subtests are intended to be measures of the specific PASS process corresponding to the scale on which they are found. The subtests are not considered to represent their own set of abilities. They do, however, have varying content (some are verbal and some not; some involve memory and others do not, etc.), but the most important point is that each is an effective measure of a specific PASS process. The *Cognitive Assessment System Administration and Scoring Manual* (Naglieri & Das, 1997b) provides a description and some discussion of each subtest on the CAS. However, the defining characteristics of the set of subtests on each scale are summarized here.

The CAS *Planning* subtests require the child to consider how to solve each item, create a plan of action, apply the plan, verify that an action taken conforms with the original goal, and modify the plan as needed. These subtests are relatively easy to perform but require the individual to make decisions about how to solve novel tasks. They also provide the examiner with the opportunity to observe strategies used by the child that can enhance interpretation of the obtained score (see Chapter 4).

All subtests included in the *Simultaneous* processing scale require the synthesis of separate elements into an interrelated group. The subtests use a variety of content (verbal and nonverbal), and some involve memory.

The *Attention* subtests require the focus of cognitive activity, detection of a particular stimulus, and inhibition of responses to competing stimuli. These subtests require examination of the features of the stimulus and a decision to respond to one and not to other competing features.

The *Successive* processing subtests involve the repetition or comprehension of the serial organization of events. All the Successive subtests require the individual to deal with information that is presented in a specific order and for which the order drives the meaning.

CONCLUSIONS

This chapter views ability testing in terms of both its strengths and limitations. The PASS theory is presented as a modern view of human cognitive processing that has been operationalized by the CAS. Evidence for the suggestions made in this chapter are provided in Chapter 5 of this volume, in the *Cognitive Assessment System Interpretive Handbook* by Naglieri and Das (1997c), and in other research previously published on the PASS theory.

🐟 TEST YOURSELF 🐟

1. Traditional IQ tests are built on the concept of general intelligence. When was that concept developed?

2. What is the main difference between traditional IQ tests and the CAS?

3. Does a person use only one of the four PASS processes at a time?

4. Which PASS process is required for repeating digits forward?
    (a) Planning
    (b) Attention
    (c) Simultaneous
    (d) Successive
    (e) All the PASS processes

5. Which PASS process is required for Block Design?
    (a) Planning
    (b) Attention
    (c) Simultaneous
    (d) Successive
    (e) All the PASS processes

6. Which PASS process is required for Object Assembly?
    (a) Planning
    (b) Attention
    (c) Simultaneous
    (d) Successive
    (e) All the PASS processes

7. From the PASS theory what does the Wechsler Verbal Scale measure?
    (a) Planning
    (b) Attention
    (c) Simultaneous
    (d) Successive
    (e) Achievement

continued

8. Which PASS processes are not assessed when using the Wechsler IQ scores?

(a) Planning

(b) Attention

(c) Simultaneous

(d) Successive

9. How does the examiner know which PASS processes are involved in a particular test or child's task?

Answers: 1. early 1900s; 2. Traditional IQ is a general view, whereas CAS offers examination of the basic building blocks of intelligence; 3. not typically; 4. d; 5. c; 6. c; 7. e; 8. a and b; 9. Analyze the demands of the task and find out what is the most important dimension. Then consider which PASS process that dimension requires. Remember also to identify which process is most critical to success.

Two

HOW TO ADMINISTER THE CAS

APPROPRIATE TESTING CONDITIONS

The CAS, like any test, must be administered and scored as prescribed in the test's *Cognitive Assessment System Administration and Scoring Manual* (Naglieri & Das, 1997b). Although it is the obligation of the user to ensure that administration procedures are consistent with applicable professional standards, it is also assumed that examiners will create an appropriate environment for administering the standardized test. Development and maintenance of rapport, for example, are critical to obtaining good data. Similarly, the importance of following directions precisely is crucial. For a description of good testing practice in general, see, for example, Aiken (1987) and Sattler (1988). The discussion that follows addresses issues that are specific to administration of the CAS.

1. **Seating Arrangement.** Proper administration of the CAS is facilitated if the examiner is within reach of the child and can closely observe the child's actions. This is especially important for the Planning subtests that involve the examiner in recording the strategies used by the child (see subsequent discussion on Strategy Assessment). Examiners would likely find sitting across from the child or across the corner of a table most appropriate for administering this instrument.

2. **Administration Directions.** The CAS instructions typically involve both verbal and nonverbal components. Examiners should carefully observe the gestures (indicated in parenthetical statements following or preceding the text of administration directions) that correspond to the oral directions. For example, the administration directions for the CAS subtest Number Detection (for children ages 8 to 17) are shown in Figure 2.1. Note that the oral instructions for the child are accompanied by directions for the examiner to point at particular times and in particular ways to the rows, numbers, and

DIRECTIONS ■ A G E S 8 – 1 7 ■

Sample C

Expose Sample C in the Response Book for Ages 8–17 and say:

> **Look at these numbers.** (Point to the rows of numbers.) **Let's find the numbers 1, 2, and 3 when they look like this** (point to the numbers following the statement "Find the numbers . . . ") **and put a line under them, like this.**

Point to the first number 4, and say

> **Here is the number 4. I won't underline that.**

Point to the number 2 at the top of the page.

> **Here is the number 2 that looks like this one, so I'll underline it.** (Demonstrate.)

Figure 2.1 Example of How Gestures and Oral Instructions Are Included in the *Cognitive Assessment System Administration and Scoring Manual*

Note. From Naglieri and Das (1997a).

sections of the Response Book. At these times examiners are instructed to "Point to each row in a sweeping motion from left to right and top to bottom" to ensure that the child understands the sequence in which the task must be completed.

3. **Administration Information.** There are two sources of information about administration of the test—the *Cognitive Assessment System Administration and Scoring Manual* and the Record Form. The same information about various administration issues is presented in a text box at the top of their respective sections. This information identifies what pages are to be used in the Response or Stimulus Books, whether a stopwatch or red pencil is needed, time limits, specific items to give, and so on. For example, Figure 2.2 shows the administration box for Matching Numbers that appears in the *Cognitive Assessment System Administration and Scoring Manual*, and Figure 2.3 shows the related box that appears in the Record Form. The fact that the information appears in two places provides examiners ample opportunity to determine how to give the subtests.

DON'T FORGET

Be sure to follow the administration directions exactly, including both the oral statements and the gestures used to guide the child's attention to the test materials.

DESCRIPTION

The child's task is to find and underline the two numbers that are the same in each row. Each item has eight rows of numbers, and each row contains six numbers. This subtest is included in the Standard and Basic Batteries.

Materials	Record Form, page 3 Response Book for Ages 5–7, pages 1–3 Response Book for Ages 8–17, pages 1–4 Red pencil Stopwatch

Administer	Ages 5–7: Demonstration, Samples A & B,
	                   Items 1–2
	Ages 8–17: Demonstration, Samples A & B,
	                   Items 2–4

Time Limits	Items 1–3: 150 seconds Item 4: 180 seconds
Record	Time in seconds Number correct Strategy Assessment

Figure 2.2 Example of Administration Box for the Matching Numbers Subtest

Note. From Naglieri and Das (1997a).

4. **Standard and Basic Batteries.** There are two versions of the CAS—a 12-subtest Standard Battery (60 minutes to give) and an 8-subtest Basic Battery (45 minutes) (see Rapid Reference on page 35). Each battery is composed of Planning, Attention, Simultaneous, and Successive subtests. If the Basic Battery is administered, the first two subtests in each of the four PASS scales are given. The subtests included in the Basic Battery are clearly noted in several ways on the Record Form and in the *Cognitive Assessment System Administration and Scoring Manual*. As shown in Figure 2.4, those subtests that form the Basic Battery are identified in dark blue boxes with white lettering on the front of the Record Form. Regardless of which version is administered, both yield PASS Scale and Full Scale standard scores with a mean of 100 and a standard deviation of 15.

Matching Numbers

Materials	Administration and Scoring Manual, pages 13–18
	Response Book for Ages 5–7, pages 1–3
	Response Book for Ages 8–17, pages 1–4
	Red Pencil
	Stopwatch
Administer	Ages 5–7: Demonstration, Samples A & B, Items 1–2
	Ages 8–17:Demonstration, Samples A & B, Items 2–4
Time Limits	See below
Record	Time in seconds
	Number correct
	Strategy Assessment

			Accuracy Score	Ratio Score (see pp. 14–16)	
Item	Time Limit	Time in seconds	(Number Correct)	Ages 5–7	Ages 8–17
All Ages ▶ Demo					

Figure 2.3 Example of Administration Box for Matching Numbers as It Appears in Record Form

Note. From Naglieri and Das (1997a).

5. **Subtest Order.** It is necessary that the CAS subtests be administered in the prescribed order to maintain the integrity of the test and reduce the influence of extraneous variables on the child's performance. The Planning, Simultaneous, Attention, and Successive order was determined to maximize the validity of the scales. The Planning subtests are administered first because they provide the fewest restrictions on how the child may complete the task. This gives the child considerable flexibility to solve the subtests in any manner. In contrast, the Attention subtests must be completed in the prescribed order (e.g., left to right, top to bottom). By administering the Planning subtests before the Attention subtests, the amount of constraint increases over time. If the Attention subtests were administered before the

Planning ones, some children might be inhibited by the more structured instruction.

The administration order of the CAS is also important if selective use of the PASS scales is considered. It is recommended that all 8 or 12 subtests be used rather than only some of the subtests, because it is not known how robust the subtests are in terms of administration order and context within which they are given. For example, Attention subtests may behave differently if they are given after another procedure that imposes procedural constraints on the child. Thus maintenance of the integrity of the CAS as a whole procedure is important.

6. **Age Partition.** Instructions and, in some cases, sets of items differ for children ages 5 to 7 and 8 to 17. This allows for tailoring of specific items to particular age groups. In addition, two Attention subtests contain different types of materials so that the content is appropriate for the two age groups. Specialized content ensures that children ages 5 to 7 can easily understand the items and that children ages 8 to 17 do not view the subtests as being too simple. For example, the Expressive Attention subtest for 5- to 7-year-olds contains pictures of animals, but the version for 8- to 17-year-olds is composed of words. The other subtest with different versions is Receptive Attention.

7. **Subtests Given by Age.** All the CAS subtests, except two, are given to all children regardless of age. The exceptions are Speech Rate, which is only administered to children ages 5 to 7, and Sentence Questions, which is only given to

Record Form
Jack A. Naglieri   J.P. Das

CAS Subtests	Raw Scores	Scaled Scores (Appendix A)				
Matching Numbers						
Planned Codes						
Planned Connections						
Nonverbal Matrices						
Verbal-Spatial Relations						
Figure Memory						
Expressive Attention						
Number Detection						
Receptive Attention						
Word Series						
Sentence Repetition						
Speech Rate/ Sentence Questions						
Sum of Subtest Scaled Scores						
		PLAN	SIM	ATT	SUC	FS
PASS Scale Standard Scores						

Figure 2.4 Example of a Blank Portion of the CAS Record Form

Note. From Naglieri and Das (1997a).

≡ *Rapid Reference*

The CAS Standard Battery consists of all 12 subtests; the Basic Battery consists of 8.

Table 2.1 Regularly Administered Items for Each CAS Subtest

Subtests (Abbreviations)	Items Given	
	Ages 5–7	Ages 8–17
Planning		
*Matching Numbers (MN)	1–2	2–4
*Planned Codes (PCd)	1–2	1–2
Planned Connections (PCn)	1–5	4–8
Simultaneous		
*Nonverbal Matrices (NvM)	1–D	7–D
*Verbal-Spatial Relations (VSR)	1–D	7–D
Figure Memory (FM)	1–D	3–D
Attention		
*Expressive Attention (EA)	1–3	4–6
*Number Detection (ND)	1–2	3–4
Receptive Attention (RA)	1–4	5–6
Successive		
*Word Series (WS)	1–D	4–D
*Sentence Repetition (SR)	1–D	1–D
Speech Rate (SpR)	1–8	—
Sentence Questions (SQ)	—	1–D

Note. D = Until discontinue rule is met.

* Subtest included in Basic Battery.

children ages 8 to 17. A list of subtests and items given is provided in Table 2.1. (This information also appears in the Record Form and *Cognitive Assessment System Administration and Scoring Manual.*) The item breakdown by age group is also reflected in the way the Record Form is constructed: The form includes boxes that are arranged so that they are filled in only when the test is given. This is shown in Figure 2.5 for Planned Connections. Note that the column labeled "Ages 5–7" has five white boxes. This indicates that in addition to the Demonstration and Sample A items, Items 1–5 are given. Similarly, the column labeled "Ages 8–17" has five white boxes that corre-

Planned Connections

Materials	Administration and Scoring Manual, pages 24–29			
	Response Book for Ages 5–7, pages 8–14			
	Response Book for Ages 8–17, pages 9–17			
	Red pencil, Stopwatch			
Administer	Ages 5–7: Demonstration, Sample A, Items 1–5			
	Ages 8–17: Sample A, Items 4–6,			
	Sample B, Items 7–8			
Time Limits	See below			
Record	Time in seconds			
	Strategy Assessment			

	Item	Time Limit	Time in seconds Ages 5–7	Time in seconds Ages 8–17
5–7 Years	Demonstration			
8–17 Years	Sample A			
	1	60" (1:00)		
			+	
	2.	60" (1:00)		
			+	
	3.	90" (1:30)		
			+	
	4.	90" (1:30)		*81*
			+	+
	5.	150" (2:30)		*121*
5–7 Stop				+
	6.	150" (2:30)		*136*
	Sample B			
				+
	7.	150" (2:30)		*142*
				+
	8.	180" (3:00)		*151*
8–17 Stop			=	=
	Raw Score			*631*
			Sum of Item 1–5, Total Seconds	Sum of Item 4–8, Total Seconds

Figure 2.5 Example of Scoring Planned Connections Items

Note. From Naglieri and Das (1997a).

spond to Items 4–8, indicating that only these items are given (in addition to the Demonstration and Sample A items).

8. **Start Rules.** Table 2.1 also shows that children ages 5 to 7 always begin with the first item but that children ages 8 to 17 typically begin with a more advanced item. The exceptions are Planned Codes (all children get the same items) and Speech Rate (all items are given to children ages 5 to 7). When a child age 8 to 17 fails the first item administered, then Item 1 is administered and testing is conducted until the discontinue rule has been met.

9. **Discontinue Rule.** Administration of some subtests is discontinued after four consecutively numbered item failures. This applies to all Simultaneous subtests and all but one of the Successive subtests (Speech Rate).

10. **Time Limits.** The time limits for items vary and for that reason are provided in the *Cognitive Assessment System Administration and Scoring Manual* and the Record Form. The limits are provided in total seconds (e.g., 150") as well as minutes and seconds (e.g., 2:30) to accommodate professionals who use digital or analog stopwatches. The point at which to begin timing is clearly indicated in the *Cognitive Assessment System Administration and Scoring Manual*. Following these instructions carefully will ensure accurate evaluation of the time the child takes to complete the items. In instances where time limits are not provided (e.g., Nonverbal Matrices), examiners should exercise good judgment when encouraging the child to attempt the next item.

11. **Rates of Presentation.** Six subtests require that stimuli be presented at a specific rate or for an exact period. One Successive subtest requires administration at the rate of one word per second (Word Series), and two subtests require a rate of two words per second (Sentence Repetition and Sentence Questions). Figure Memory involves stimuli that are presented for exactly five seconds, and in the Verbal-Spatial Relations subtest there is a 30-second exposure time limit for each item. Time limits must be followed exactly to allow comparison to the normative sample.

12. **Strategy Assessment.** All the CAS Planning subtests include an observational phase called Strategy Assessment: The examiner observes if the child uses strategies to complete the items. Strategy Assessment was developed to obtain information about how the child completes the items; it is used to help describe the standard scores that are obtained (see Chapter 4). This information allows the examiner to look beyond the score and understand the methods the child used during planning. The specific strategy used is interpreted in relation

to the standard score and the percentage of children who used that strategy in the standardization sample. This may help explain a particularly high or low Planning score and can be integrated into the overall pool of data that constitutes the entire evaluation.

Rapid Reference

Strategy Assessment is conducted at the end of administration of all Planning subtests except Planned Codes, where it is conducted after each of the two items.

Strategy Assessment includes two parts—Observed Strategies and Reported Strategies. Observed Strategies are those seen by the examiner through nonobtrusive means while the child completes the items. Examiners often evaluate how children complete test items through careful observation during testing. Reported Strategies are obtained following completion of the item(s) of each Planning subtest. The examiner obtains this information by saying "Tell me how you did these" or "How did you find what you were looking for?" or making a similar statement. The strategies can be communicated by the child through either verbal or nonverbal (gesturing) means. (See Rapid Reference above.)

To facilitate recording of strategies that are both "Observed" and "Reported," a Strategy Assessment Checklist is included in the appropriate sections of the Record Form (see Figure 2.6). Examiners indicate which strategy or strategies were used by placing a check mark in the appropriate location(s) during the observation and reporting stages. Unique strategies may be recorded in the space provided.

13. **Provide Help Guidelines.** The instructions for administration of the CAS were written to ensure that the child understands the demands of every subtest. Several methods were used to achieve this: sample and demon-

Strategy Assessment Checklist		
Obs	**Rep**	**Description of Strategy**
		1. Looked at first then last digits
		2. Looked at first then last digit
		3. Looked at first two digits
✓	✓	4. Looked at the last number
		5. Looked at the first digit
		6. Put finger on the number
✓		7. Verbalized the number
		8. Scanned the row for a match
		9. No strategy

Other:
Observed _____

Reported _____

Figure 2.6 Example of How the Strategy Assessment Checklist May Be Used

Note. From Naglieri and Das (1997a).

DON'T FORGET

Be sure to observe strategy use when the child completes the Planning Scale subtests.

stration items, as well as opportunities for the examiner to clarify the requirements of the task. For example, after the first sample item in Expressive Attention, the child is asked if he or she is ready to begin. If the child does not seem ready or appears in any way confused or uncertain, the examiner is instructed to "provide a brief explanation if necessary." This instruction is intended to give the examiner the freedom to explain what the child must do in whatever terms are considered necessary in order to ensure that the child understands the task. The interaction can be in any form including gestures, verbal statement, or communication in any language. The intent of this instruction is to give the examiner full authority in making clear the demands of the subtest and to allow the examiner to be certain that the child is well informed about what to do. The instruction is not intended to teach the child how to do the test, but rather to tell the child what is required. (See Rapid Reference below.)

14. **Bilingual or Hearing-Impaired Children.** The CAS administration instructions were designed to give the examiner flexibility to interact with the child to ensure that good data are obtained. It is assumed that the child has an adequate working knowledge of English so that he or she will benefit from the samples and demonstrations provided. However, it is possible to augment the English instructions when the statement "provide additional help when needed" is given. That is, during introductory portions of the subtests examiners who have the knowledge to interact with the child in his or her native language or through another means such as sign language may do so when instructed to provide assistance. The

≡ *Rapid Reference*

Provide Help Guidelines allow the examiner to restate the subtest directions in any language or any manner to ensure that the child understands the demands of the task.

• The examiner can explain the task in his or her own words.

• Directions can be given in any language.

• Directions can be given non-verbally.

• Provide Help is *not* a teaching of the test, but rather an explanation of what is required.

child's need for information in another language or through another method can become obvious (a) when the child asks for help by using another language, (b) if it is apparent that the child is hearing impaired, or (c) if the child does not respond to the instruction. In such instances it is the responsibility of the examiner to decide when to use another method of communication. It is also the responsibility of the examiner to acknowledge when he or she does not know the child's other language, and, therefore, determine that another examiner should evaluate the child or an interpreter should be used.

15. **Spoiled Subtests.** It is possible that one of the three regularly administered subtests in the Standard Battery may be spoiled. In such an instance, examiners could use the remaining two subtests and compute the PASS Scale score using the Basic Battery norms. Alternatively, the prorated values provided in Table 3.2 (page 65) can be used. In either case the Full Scale requires either 8 or 12 subtest scores for the Basic and Standard Batteries, respectively.

KEY POINTS TO REMEMBER FOR ACCURATE ADMINISTRATION

It is important to consider certain issues when administering each of the CAS subtests. This discussion is organized by subtest in the order of administration.

Matching Numbers

The child's task in this subtest is to find and underline two numbers that are the same in each row. Each item is composed of eight rows of numbers, with six numbers per row. Two of the six numbers in each row are the same. The length of numbers differs on the various rows. Numbers increase in length from one digit on the first row of Item 1 to seven digits on the eighth row of Item 4. There are four rows for each digit length and a total of four pages of numbers. Each row of numbers was carefully developed to maximize benefits of strategy usage in the identification of correct matches. This approach resulted in items with some rows that contain numbers starting with unique numbers, some rows that include numbers with similar digit strings, and some rows in which the first numbers are more similar than those at the end of the row.

Administration Comments:

- The examiner should always fold back the Response Book so that the child sees only one page at a time.
- When necessary, it is permissible to remind the child to indicate when he or she is finished by saying "Tell me when you're finished."
- Although the child may self-correct, do not allow the child to spend more than a second or two crossing out. If the child takes too much time, say "Keep going."
- Sometimes children stop before the time limit has expired. If necessary, the examiner should say "Keep going."
- Strategy Assessment is conducted during and at the end of this subtest. Be sure to fill in the Strategy Assessment Checklist on the Record Form.

Planned Codes

This subtest contains two items, each with its own set of codes and particular arrangements of rows and columns. A legend at the top of each page shows which letters correspond to which codes (e.g., A, B, C, D with OX, XX, OO, XO, respectively). Just below the legend are seven rows and eight columns of letters without the codes. Children write the corresponding codes in boxes beneath each of the letters. The items differ in the correspondence of letters to codes and the position of the letters on the page. In the first item, the letters appear in columns for A, B, C, and D. That is, all the As appear in the first column, all the Bs in the second column, all the Cs in the third column, and so on. On the second item, the letters are configured in a diagonal pattern.

Administration Comments:

- The child may fill in the boxes in any order and in fact is instructed, "You can do it any way you want" (p. 21). This allows the child to use strategies such as doing all the As first or completing the page by skipping around.
- Although self-corrections are permitted, children are discouraged from spending more than a second or two erasing. If necessary, the examiner should say "Keep going." Similarly, if the child stops prior

to the expiration of the time limit, the examiner instructs the child to keep going.

- Strategy Assessment is conducted in this subtest for each item or page separately because different strategies are used on the two versions.

Planned Connections

This subtest contains two types of items. The first six items require children to connect numbers in sequential order. The last two items require children to connect both numbers and letters in sequential order, alternating between numbers and letters (e.g., 1-A-2-B-3-C). If the child makes a mistake, the examiner directs the child back to the previous correct position. Children ages 5 to 7 are administered Items 1 through 5. Children ages 8 to 17 are administered Items 4 through 8. The items are constructed so that children never complete a sequence by crossing one line over the other. This provides a means of reducing the areas to be searched when looking for the next number or letter.

Administration Comments:

- There are two important points about starting each Planned Connections item. First, timing begins when the examiner says "Now do this one. Begin here," and points to the number 1. Second, the examiner always tells the child where to begin by pointing to the number 1.

- It is imperative that children complete the sequence correctly; therefore errors are corrected immediately. An error is defined as the connection of two boxes that are not in correct sequence. If the child makes an error, the examiner is instructed to immediately say "Wait, you made a mistake. Begin again from here" (and point to the previous correct location). Instructions do not allow the child to erase an error because the timing does not stop during this instruction.

- In order to correct the child as the task is being completed, the examiner must be able to keep track of the child's progress. This is not too difficult when the items are numbers in sequence, but it becomes more complicated when the items involve alternating num-

DON'T FORGET

Be sure to point to the number 1 in each Planned Connections item so the child knows where to begin.

bers and letters. The best way to score these items as the child progresses is for the examiner to use a "look back" strategy. For example, if the child is on the letter D, the examiner looks back to the previous point (the number 3) and then instantly knows that the number 4 follows the letter D.

- Occasionally a child may stop before reaching the last number or letter. In such instances, the examiner must immediately say "Keep going."

Nonverbal Matrices

Nonverbal Matrices is a 33-item multiple choice subtest. Each item utilizes geometric shapes and elements that are interrelated through spatial or logical organization. Children are required to decode the relationships among the parts of the item and choose the best of six options. The Nonverbal Matrices subtest items are composed of a variety of formats including completion of geometric patterns, reasoning by analogy, and spatial visualization included in the Matrix Analogies Test (Naglieri, 1985) and its revision, the Naglieri Nonverbal Ability Test (Naglieri, 1997b).

Administration Comments:

- This subtest has a starting rule (Item 7) for children ages 8 to 17. If the child age 8 to 17 fails Item 7, the examiner goes back to Item 1 and uses the directions for the age 5–7 group. Children ages 5 to 7 and older children with suspected cognitive disability begin with Item 1.
- It is important to note that for the sample and first items that are given, the examiner tells the child the answer whether the child is correct or not. This ensures that all children receive the same information about the item.
- Discontinue after four consecutively numbered items are failed.

Verbal-Spatial Relations

This subtest is composed of items that require the comprehension of logical and grammatical descriptions of spatial relationships. Children are presented with items with six drawings and a printed question at the bottom of each page. The examiner reads the question aloud, and the child selects the option that matches the verbal description. The items require the evaluation of logical grammatical relationships, which demands Simultaneous processing with verbal content.

Administration Comments:

- The examiner always reads every question printed at the bottom of the page, even if the child is capable of reading it alone.
- The examiner should read the questions in a very clear manner, in a normal reading voice, at the rate of about two words per second.
- Each question can only be read once.
- Timing begins when the item is exposed, and timing ends when the child completes the item or when the time limit expires.
- If a child age 8 to 17 fails Item 7, give Item 1 and use the directions for the age 5–7 group. Then administer forward until the discontinue rule has been met. Children ages 5 to 7 and older children with suspected cognitive disability begin with Item 1.
- If a child fails four consecutive items, discontinue the subtest.
- There is a 30-second time limit. If a child does not respond in that time, score the item 0 (failed) and go on to the next item if appropriate.
- The items are printed at the bottom of each page in the Stimulus Book, and they also appear in the *Cognitive Assessment System Administration and Scoring Manual* following instructions for the subtest.

Figure Memory

The child's task is to identify a two- or three-dimensional geometric figure that is shown for 5 seconds when it is embedded within a more complex design.

Children are asked to identify the original figure that is embedded within the larger design. The child reproduces the figure on the response page by drawing over the lines with a red pencil. For a response to be scored as correct, all lines of the design must be indicated without any additions or omissions.

Administration Comments:

- Children ages 5 to 7 and older children with suspected cognitive disability begin with Item 1, and those ages 8 to 17 start with Item 3. If a child age 8 to 17 fails Item 3, give Item 1 using the directions for the age 5–7 group and administer forward until the discontinue rule has been met.
- The discontinue rule is four consecutively numbered items failed.
- The exposure time for each item is 5 seconds.
- The sequence of administration is as follows:

  1. Examiners should place the Stimulus Book in front of the child so the bottom edge of the book (as seen by the child) is 7 to 8 inches from the edge of the table. This allows for placement of the Response Book between the child and the Stimulus Book.
  2. Expose each stimulus figure for exactly 5 seconds.
  3. Then turn the stimulus page to remove the item from the child's view.
  4. Next, immediately place the appropriate page of the Response Book in front of the child.
  5. Then remove the Response Book after the child has responded.
  6. Begin the sequence again for the next item.

- During the sample and Item 1, it is permissible to clarify the directions by using another word, such as *trace*.
- Sometimes it is necessary to communicate to the child that self-corrections are permitted. Examiners are free to explain that corrections can be made by either crossing out or erasing.
- The examiner must score the child's responses during the administration so that the discontinue rule can be determined. To assist the examiner, the answers for the demonstration and sample items as well as for all the remaining items appear in the *Cognitive Assessment System Administration and Scoring Manual.* Note that the diagrams are presented as seen by the child (the view that would also be seen by

the examiner sitting next to the child) and as seen by the examiner (if the examiner is sitting across from the child).

Expressive Attention

Expressive Attention consists of two different types of items. The first is administered to children ages 5 to 7. The child's task is to identify the pictures of animals as either large or small, regardless of their relative size on the page. There are three pages of animal pictures (each page is considered an item). In the first item all the animals are the same size. In the second the animals are sized relative to actual size. The third item is the most sensitive to Attention because the animals are usually sized opposite to their actual size.

The second set of items is administered to children ages 8 to 17. There are also three items in this version. First, the child reads words such as *blue* and *yellow*; second, the child identifies colors of a group of rectangles; finally, the child identifies the color ink in which certain words are printed. It is the last page that is sensitive to Attention because here the child has to focus on one variable (the color) and not read the word (a more automatic response).

Administration Comments:

- Even though all three items in the appropriate item set are administered to each child, only the last item is considered a measure of Attention.
- If a child makes more than five errors on Sample A, or cannot read, or has difficulty seeing the colors, do not administer the subtest.
- Synonyms for the words *big* and *small* (e.g., *large* or *little*) are acceptable. Similarly, if a child calls the bird a robin or a blue jay, say "Yes, and it's a bird."
- Unlike Planning subtests that can be completed in any manner, all Attention subtests require that the child complete each item row by row, from left to right, and from top to bottom. If the child deviates, the examiner must immediately say "Do it this way" (point across the rows from the child's left to right).
- Self-corrections are permitted on this subtest and are scored as correct. They do, however, increase the time taken and therefore influence the child's score.

DON'T FORGET

The demonstration item for Expressive Attention for children ages 5 to 7 is designed to ensure that they know or can learn which animals are big and which are small. Don't forget to go through the demonstration carefully and provide a brief explanation if necessary.

- Timing begins when the child says the first word, and timing ends when the child says the last word.

Number Detection

This subtest consists of items (pages) of rows of numbers that contain both targets (numbers that match the stimuli) and distractors (numbers that do not match the stimuli). The child's task is to underline numbers on a page that match stimuli at the top of the page.

Administration Comments:

- In contrast to Planning subtests, which allow the child to choose a method to complete the page, this subtest must be competed row by row, from left to right, and from top to bottom. If the child deviates, the examiner must say "Do it this way" (point across the rows from the child's left to right). Similarly, if the child skips a row, the examiner must immediately say "Do this row first" (point to the skipped row). These instructions block the child's application of plans.
- After completion of the page, some children may want to go back and check their work (a good plan). However, because this test is designed to measure Attention, do not allow the child to review or modify responses after completing the page.
- Because time is an important variable in this test, if the child indicates a desire to change a response, say "Cross out your mistake and keep going." This encourages rapid completion of the page.
- Timing begins when each item (page) is exposed and the instruction "Begin" is given.

Receptive Attention

The child's task is to find and underline pairs of pictures or pairs of letters that are the same on each item (page). Each item consists of rows of pictures or letters that contain both targets (pairs that match) and distractors (pairs that do not match). For children ages 5 to 7, the picture pairs match on the basis of either physical appearance or category (name). For the age 8–17 group, the child must underline pairs of letters that are physically the same or have the same name.

Administration Comments:

- The child must complete the task row by row, from left to right, and from top to bottom. If the child deviates, say "Do it this way" (point across the rows from the child's left to right).
- If necessary, instruct the child not to spend too much time drawing the lines neatly.
- Do not allow the child to review or modify responses after completing the page.
- Timing begins when each item (page) is exposed and the instruction "Begin" is given.

Word Series

The child's task is to repeat a series of single-syllable, high-imagery words in the same order in which the examiner says them.

Administration Comments:

- The words are presented in a uniform pitch at the rate of one word per second.
- The examiner must drop his or her voice when the last word of the series is spoken, so that the child knows when the presentation is complete.
- Mispronunciations (e.g., *Tee* for *Key*) and word ending changes are not counted as errors.
- Discontinue the subtest if a child fails four consecutively numbered items.
- Children ages 8 to 17 begin with Item 4. If a child in this age group fails Item 4, give Item 1 (using the directions for the age 5–7 group) and administer forward until the discontinue rule has been met.
- During the introduction of the test, the examiner tells the child all the words that are used.

Sentence Repetition

The child's task is to repeat a series of sentences spoken by the examiner. Each sentence contains color names in place of content words.

Administration Comments:

- The examiner reads the sentences in a normal reading voice, at the rate of about two words per second.
- The examiner uses normal intonation and drops his or her voice when the last word of every sentence is spoken, or at the end of phrases.
- The longer sentences contain commas, which indicate how the words should be grouped.
- Each sentence is read one time only.
- When the child fails four consecutively numbered items, the subtest is discontinued.
- The items appear in the *Cognitive Assessment System Administration and Scoring Manual* and the Record Form.

Speech Rate (Ages 5 to 7 Only)

This subtest requires the child to say a series of words as fast as possible 10 times. Each of the eight items contains a series of one- or two-syllable words that demand repetition of a sequence of sounds.

Administration Comments:

- The examiner reads the words in a normal reading voice at the rate of about two words per second.
- The examiner counts the number of times the child repeats the sequence of words until the three-word sequence has been said 10 times. Examiners keep track of how many times the sequence has been repeated by placing a mark on the Record Form for each correct repetition.

CAUTION

Be sure to read the items for Sentence Repetition, Sentence Questions, and Verbal-Spatial Relations in a normal reading voice at about the rate of two words per second.

- The 10 repetitions do not have to be consecutive. That is, if the child says the three words correctly five times, then makes a mistake, then says the three words correctly five times, the task is competed and the total time is measured. Thus any repetition in which the child makes an error is not counted.
- If the child stops before completing 10 repetitions of the series, the examiner must immediately say "Keep going until I tell you to stop."
- If the child makes several errors or is unable to continue the series, stop and re-administer the item. Attempt to administer the item up to three times, in which case the subtest must be considered spoiled.
- An error is any change in the sequence of the three-word phrase or any incomplete repetition of the three-word phrase.
- Mispronunciations, distortions, and other articulation difficulties are not counted as errors. For example, in the sequence "man-cow-key," if the child says "man-cow-key, man-cow-key, man-cow-dee, man-cow-key," all these responses would be counted. However, if the child cannot say the words in a recognizable manner, do not administer the subtest.
- Timing begins when the child says the first word for the first time, and timing ends when the child says the last word for the 10th time.

Sentence Questions (Ages 8 to 17 Only)

The child's task is to answer a question about a sentence read by the examiner. Each sentence is in the same format as items on the Sentence Repetition subtest and contains color names in place of content words.

Administration Comments:

- The examiner reads the items in a normal reading voice at the rate of about two words per second.
- The examiner uses normal intonation and drops his or her voice when the last word of every sentence is spoken, or at the end of phrases.
- The longer sentences contain commas, which indicate how the words should be grouped.

- If the child requests that the sentence and question be repeated, the examiner may do so, but only once.
- If a child fails four consecutive items, the subtest is discontinued.

CONCLUSIONS

Readers should reference the *Cognitive Assessment System Administration and Scoring Manual* for more information and specific instructions for giving the subtests. Although the test was written to be easy to administer, as with any new test it is expected that the initial administration will require some attention to the details described in this chapter. After a few administrations, however, examiners will become more comfortable with the procedures.

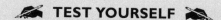

TEST YOURSELF

1. **What is the discontinue rule for the Simultaneous and most Successive subtests?**
   (a) 2
   (b) 3
   (c) 4
   (d) 5 consecutively numbered errors
2. **What is the rate of presentation for Word Series?**
   (a) 1
   (b) 2
   (c) 3 words per second
3. **What is the rate of presentation for Sentence Repetition, Sentence Questions, and Verbal-Spatial Relations?**
   (a) 1
   (b) 2
   (c) 3 words per second
4. **What is the exposure time for Figure Memory items?**
   (a) 2
   (b) 3
   (c) 4
   (d) 5 seconds

5. **What age group is administered Speech Rate?**

   (a) 5 to 7

   (b) 8 to 17

   (c) all ages

6. **What age group is administered Sentence Questions?**

   (a) 5 to 7

   (b) 8 to 17

   (c) all ages

7. **When does the examiner start timing the child on the Expressive Attention subtest?**

   (a) when the page is exposed

   (b) when the directions are completed

   (c) when the child says the first word

8. **Should the examiner change the order of administration of CAS subtests?**

   (a) It is permissible.

   (b) It is not advised.

9. **How many subtests do the Standard and Basic CAS batteries have?**

   (a) 12 and 10

   (b) 12 and 8

   (c) 8 and 4

   (d) 10 and 8

10. **About how long do the Standard and Basic CAS batteries take to administer?**

   (a) 60" and 30"

   (b) 45" and 30"

   (c) 60" and 45"

   (d) 45" and 20"

Answers: 1. c; 2. b; 3. b; 4. d; 5. a; 6. b; 7. c; 8. b; 9. b; 10. c

Three

Threhe CAS is scored by using methods that should be well known to the experienced practitioner. Essentially, the sequence of events follows this pattern:

1. Subtest raw scores are obtained.
2. Raw scores are converted to subtest scaled scores.
3. PASS Scale standard scores are obtained from the sum of the respective subtest scaled scores.
4. The CAS Full Scale score is obtained from the sum of all subtest scaled scores.

CALCULATING SUBTEST RAW SCORES

The CAS subtest raw scores are calculated by using four different methods based on the particular aspects of the child's performance that are being measured. These methods include one or more of the following dimensions: (a) the number correct, (b) time to completion, and (c) number of false detections. The methods of evaluating a child's performance are used either in isolation or in combination based on the goals of the subtest. Some subtest raw scores, therefore, are based on (a) number correct, (b) total time, (c) number correct and total time, and (d) number correct, total time, and number of false detections.

Number Correct

The raw score for the Nonverbal Matrices, Verbal-Spatial Relations, Figure Memory, Word Series, Sentence Repetition, and Sentence Questions subtests is the number of items correct. This score is obtained by summing the number of correct items and assigning credit for those items not administered below any starting point. There are some important variations and scoring rules for these subtests.

Nonverbal Matrices and Verbal-Spatial Relations

These subtests are very straightforward. The child earns a score of 1 if the correct option is selected. Although the Nonverbal Matrices subtest does not have a time limit for each item, there is a 30-second time limit for exposure of the Verbal-Spatial Relations items. If the child does not respond within that time, the item is scored as failed. The raw score for both subtests is the sum of the number correct (giving credit for items not administered below the starting point when appropriate).

Figure Memory items are also scored as 1 or 0. To receive credit, the child must draw a red line on each of the lines that make up the figure. The child does not, however, have to draw the lines precisely as long as each of the lines of the figure is drawn. This is illustrated in Figure 3.1. Notice that in the response scored as 0 the child did not draw a line on the bottom of the square. That is, instead of drawing five lines as required (the four sides of the box and the diagonal), the child only produced four lines (three sides of the box and the diagonal).

Examiners must score the child's responses to Figure Memory during administration in order to determine if the discontinue rule has been met. To facilitate scoring, the *Cognitive Assessment System Administration and Scoring Manual* (Naglieri & Das, 1997b) includes diagrams of the Response Book page with the correct answer indicated as it would be

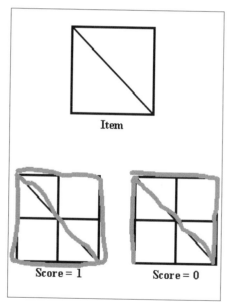

Figure 3.1 Scoring Figure Memory Responses

seen from both the child's and examiner's perspective. If the examiner is sitting across from the child, the part of the manual that shows the examiner's view should be used. Similarly, if the examiner is sitting next to or diagonally across from the child, the section of the manual that shows the correct answer from the child's perspective will be most helpful. (See Rapid Reference below.)

> ## DON'T FORGET
>
> - There is a 30-second time limit for exposure of each Verbal-Spatial Relations item. Begin timing when the page is exposed. The time it takes the examiner to read the question is included in the timing of the item.
>
> - Figure Memory items are exposed for exactly 5 seconds, but there is no time limit on how long the child has to respond.

Word Series, Sentence Repetition, and Sentence Questions

The raw score for Word Series is the number of items correctly repeated. To earn a score of 1, the child must reproduce the entire string of words (e.g., "book-key-wall") in the correct order. The child is scored 0 if the order is changed in any manner or if a word is deleted from the item. Mispronunciations of the words and word distortions, however, are not counted as errors.

Sentence Repetition and Sentence Questions

Although Sentence Repetition and Sentence Questions subtests are scored as Pass or Fail, the way the items are scored varies. In Sentence Repetition the child must repeat the entire sentence exactly as stated by the examiner. Any inaccuracies such as word substitutions, omissions, additions, reversals, and changes in word endings are considered errors and result in a score of 0 for the item. Mispronunciations such as "wed" for "red," however, are not counted as errors.

Sentence Questions items are also scored either Pass (1) or Fail (0), but the rules are very different.

> ## Rapid Reference
>
> Answers to the Figure Memory items appear on pages 47–50 of the *Cognitive Assessment System Administration and Scoring Manual*. These answers are printed in two orientations—as seen by the child, and as seen by the examiner sitting across from the child.

Item: The yellow purples are red and the whites are green.

Question: Who are red?

Answer as shown in Record Form: (The) yellow purple(s)

Answers that receive a score of 1 (pass):

    "The yellow purples"

    "The yellow purple"

    "Yellow purple"

    "Yellow purples"

Figure 3.2 Answers That Are Scored 1 for Sentence Questions

The *Cognitive Assessment System Administration and Scoring Manual* and the Record Form each contain the items and a list of possible correct answers. The possible answers are shown in parentheses that indicate those parts of the answers that are not required. The examiner scores the items according to whether the child produces all the words or word fragments that are not included within parentheses. This is illustrated in Figure 3.2. Note that any combination of words or word endings that are contained within the parentheses can be omitted or added. What is essential for a score of 1 is the response "yellow purple" *in that order.* That is, if the child says "purple yellow," then the item is failed.

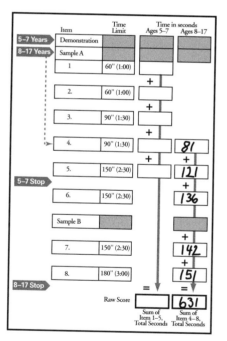

Figure 3.3 Item Scores for Planned Connections

Note. From Naglieri and Das (1997a).

Total Time (in seconds)

The raw score for Planned Connections and Speech Rate is the sum of the time in seconds to complete all items. To compute the raw score, simply add the time scores for the items administered. An illustration of this procedure is provided for Planned Connections in Figure 3.3 (use the same method to obtain the raw score for Speech Rate). Figure 3.3 shows calculation of the raw score for a child age 9 years 0 months.

Accuracy (Total Time and Number Correct)

CAUTION

Remember that when you are using a digital stopwatch and have item time scores that are greater than 1 minute, you have to add 60 seconds for each minute to the number of seconds. Convert scores in minutes:seconds to total seconds (e.g., a score of 1:20 is recorded as 80 seconds). Sum the item times in total seconds for Planned Connections and Speech Rate to get the subtest raw scores.

The raw score for the Matching Numbers, Planned Codes, and Expressive Attention subtests is based on the combination of time and number correct. First, time is recorded in total seconds for each item; then the number correct per item is determined (this is best accomplished for Matching Numbers by using the Scoring Templates described later in this chapter). The number correct and time for each item on these subtests are combined into a ratio score. The number correct for Matching Numbers, Planned Codes, and Expressive Attention is called Accuracy in the conversion table that appears on pages 14–16 of the Record Form.

The Ratio Score Conversion Table included in the Record Form and shown in Figure 3.4 includes a heading called Accuracy Score. The farthest left column contains time scores in 3-second intervals. To combine the number correct and time into a ratio score, enter the row that contains the item time in seconds and then find the column for the Accuracy Score earned by the child. The number at the intersection of the row and column is the ratio score for that item. For example, if a child earns a total time score of 43 seconds with an Accuracy Score of 38, then the ratio score is 54.

The ratio scores for each item are summed, as indicated on the Record Form, to obtain a raw score for each subtest. An illustration is given for Matching Numbers in Figure 3.5 (use the same method to obtain the raw scores for Planned Codes and Expressive Attention). Note that the age of

| TIME (seconds) | Ratio Score Conversion Table C | | | | | | | | | | | |
| | Accuracy Score: Number Correct (MN, PCd, EA) or Number Cor... | | | | | | | | | | | |
	37	38	39	40	41	42	43	44	45	46	47	48
0–2	200	200	200	200	200	200	200	200	200	200	200	200
3–5	200	200	200	200	200	200	200	200	200	200	200	200
6–8	200	200	200	200	200	200	200	200	200	200	200	200
9–11	200	200	200	200	200	200	200	200	200	200	200	200
12–14	170	177	185	192	200	200	200	200	200	200	200	200
15–17	138	144	150	156	163	169	176	182	189	196	200	200
18–20	116	121	126	132	137	142	148	153	159	165	171	177
21–23	100	105	109	114	118	123	128	133	138	143	148	153
24–26	88	92	96	100	104	108	112	117	121	125	130	135
27–29	79	82	86	89	93	97	100	104	108	112	116	120
30–32	71	74	77	81	84	87	91	94	98	101	105	109
33–35	65	68	71	74	77	80	83	86	89	92	96	99
36–38	60	62	65	68	70	73	76	79	82	85	88	91
39–41	55	58	60	63	65	68	70	73	76	78	81	84
42–44	51	54	56	58	60	63	65	68	70	73	76	78
45–47	48	50	52	54	57	59	61	63	66	68	71	73
48–50	45	47	49	51	53	55	57	60	62	64	66	69

Figure 3.4 Ratio Score Conversion Table Example

Note. From Naglieri and Das (1997a).

the child is irrelevant, as all children's scores are converted to ratio scores based on time and accuracy. Expressive Attention Items 1 and 2 (ages 5 to 7) and 4 and 5 (ages 8 to 17) are *not* included in the computation of the subtest raw score. These pages prepare the child for the last page given (pp. 3 and 6 for the 5–7 and 8–17 age groups, respectively). The last page is used to evaluate the child's attention.

Determination of the number correct for Matching Numbers and Planned Codes is facilitated by using a scoring guide included in the spiral-bound Scoring Templates booklet. Place the completed Response Book under the appropriate template (the book is divided into sections for children ages 5 to 7 and 8 to 17). Align the page completed by the child with the scoring template (see Figure 3.6). The template is a translucent paper that contains the correct answers and allows for easy determination of the number correct for the item. Record the number correct for each item in the Accuracy Score column of the Record Form. Because the child responds orally to the Expressive Attention items, this subtest does not require the use of a template.

Accuracy (Total Time, Number Correct, and False Detections)

The raw scores for Number Detection and Receptive Attention are also obtained by using ratio scores, but the Accuracy Score is defined differently for these subtests. Accuracy is the number of correct responses (i.e., underlined targets) minus the number of false detections (the number of times the child underlined a stimulus that is not a target). The Scoring Templates booklet is used to identify how many targets (what the child is instructed to look for) and false detections the child responded to, as described earlier in

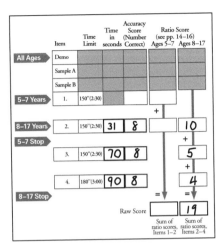

Figure 3.5 Calculation of Ratio Scores for Matching Numbers Subtest

Note. From Naglieri and Das (1997a).

this chapter (see Figure 3.6). In addition to counting the number of correct answers (targets that appear in circles), the examiner should count the number of non-targets underlined (false detections). Subtract the number of false detections from the number correct to obtain the Accuracy Score. Then convert the time and Accuracy Scores to a ratio score in the usual fashion as described earlier. This is illustrated for Number Detection (use the same method to obtain the raw score for Receptive Attention) in Figure 3.7.

CONVERTING RAW SCORES TO SUBTEST SCALED SCORES

The CAS subtest scaled scores (mean of 10 and standard deviation of 3) are obtained by using age-based tables included in Appendix A.1 (pages 99–177) of the *Cognitive Assessment System Administration and Scoring Manual*. The Appendix is divided according to the child's chronological age in years, months, and days. Locate the appropriate conversion table (the first page of the subtest norms section includes an index showing which pages in the manual apply to each age group).

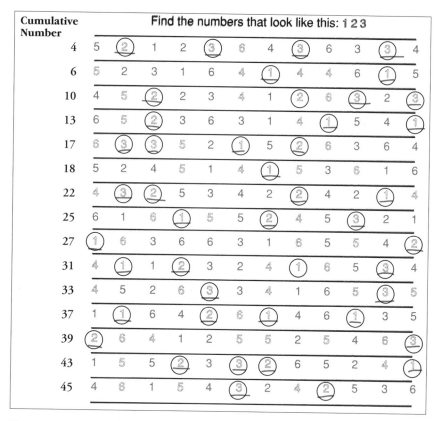

Figure 3.6 Using the Scoring Template to Score Number Detection

Note. From Naglieri and Das (1997a).

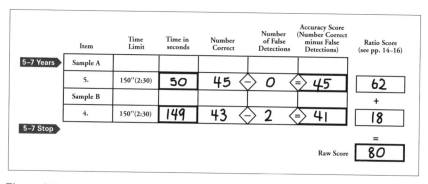

Figure 3.7 Calculation of Ratio Scores for the Number Detection Subtest

Note. From Naglieri and Das (1997a).

DERIVING PASS SCALE STANDARD SCORES FROM THE SUM OF SUBTEST SCALED SCORES

Each of the four PASS Scale scores is derived from the sum of the subtest scaled scores. For the Standard Battery, sum all three subtest scaled scores within each PASS scale. For the Basic Battery, sum only the first two subtests within each PASS scale. The Full Scale score is obtained from the sum of scaled scores for both the Standard and Basic Batteries and is calculated by summing the four "Sum of Subtest Scaled Scores" values found on the front page of the Record Form. (See Figure 3.8.)

Note that the section on the front page of the CAS Record Form contains information about which subtests are included in the Basic Battery. For example, the Basic Battery subtests appear as white type in a dark blue background.

OBTAINING PASS SCALE STANDARD SCORES

The PASS Scale scores (mean of 100 and standard deviation of 15) are derived from the sum of subtest scaled scores by using Appendix B (pages 179–191) of the *Cognitive Assessment System Administration and Scoring Manual* (Naglieri & Das, 1997b). Tables B.1 to B.5 are used to obtain scores for the Standard Battery, and Tables B.6 to B.10 for the Basic Battery. Each PASS scale has its own table. The table provides the standard score, percentile, and confidence intervals (90% and 95%). Note that the confidence intervals are the estimated true score type (see *Cognitive Assessment System Interpretive Handbook* [Naglieri & Das, 1997c] for more information).

If a subtest is spoiled when the 12-subtest Standard Battery is being administered, the practitioner has two options. One is to revert back to the 8-subtest Basic Battery version for calculation of the PASS and Full Scale standard scores. Another option is to prorate the sum of three subtest scaled scores from the sum of the two that were

> ## DON'T FORGET
>
> Convert the sum of scaled scores for the PASS and Full Scale standard scores by using two subtests per scale for the Basic Battery and three for the Standard Battery. Be sure to consult the appropriate conversion tables when looking up these scores.

Record Form

Jack A. Naglieri   J.P. Das

CAS Subtests	Raw Scores	Scaled Scores (Appendix A)				
Matching Numbers	4	6				
Planned Codes	25	8				
Planned Connections	412	6				
Nonverbal Matrices	13		10			
Verbal-Spatial Relations	14		9			
Figure Memory	9		10			
Expressive Attention	28			9		
Number Detection	34			10		
Receptive Attention	37			12		
Word Series	10				10	
Sentence Repetition	8				11	
Speech Rate/ Sentence Questions	9				10	
Sum of Subtest Scaled Scores		20	29	31	31	111
		PLAN	SIM	ATT	SUC	FS
PASS Scale Standard Scores (Appendix B)		79	98	102	102	93
Percentile Rank (Appendix B)		8	45	55	55	32
____ % Confidence Intervals (Appendix B) Lower		74	92	94	95	88
Upper		89	105	109	108	98

Figure 3.8 Completing the CAS Record Form

Note. From Naglieri and Das (1997a).

not spoiled. Then a sum of subtest scaled scores for the spoiled PASS scale can be obtained by using only two subtests. Table 3.1 can be used to obtain an estimated sum of subtest scores for this purpose. To use this table, find in the first (left-hand) column the sum of the scaled scores for the two subtests. Then read across the table to obtain the estimated sum of three subtests based on the sum of the two. This value is used to obtain the appropriate Planning, Simultaneous, Attention, and Successive Scale standard scores. Use the prorated sum of scaled scores when summing the PASS scores to obtain the Full Scale score.

If one of the Basic Battery subtests is spoiled during administration, practitioners have the option to give the last subtest on the scale. That subtest scaled score could be used as one of the two scores needed to obtain a Basic Battery sum of scaled scores and the Full Scale score. This practice should be limited to those rare instances in which limitations demand variation from the normally prescribed method of calculating scores for the Basic Battery.

OBTAINING FULL SCALE STANDARD SCORES

The CAS Full Scale score (mean of 100 and standard deviation of 15) is obtained from the sum of the scaled scores used to obtain the four PASS Scale

Table 3.1 Prorated Sums of Scaled Scores for PASS Scales

Sum of two subtest scaled scores	Estimated sum of three pro-rated scores	Sum of two subtest scaled scores	Estimated sum of three pro-rated scores
2	3	22	33
3	5	23	35
4	6	24	36
5	8	25	38
6	9	26	39
7	11	27	41
8	12	28	42
9	14	29	44
10	15	30	45
11	17	31	47
12	18	32	48
13	20	33	50
14	21	34	51
15	23	35	53
16	24	36	54
17	26	37	56
18	27	38	57
19	29	39	59
20	30	40	60
21	32		

scores by using Appendix B (pages 179–191) of the *Cognitive Assessment System Administration and Scoring Manual.* The Full Scale score is computed from the sum of 8 or 12 subtests if the Basic and Standard Batteries, respectively, are given. The sum of the subtest scaled scores, which appears on the front of the Record Form, is used to obtain the standard score. Like the PASS con-

≡ *Rapid Reference*

The percentile ranks and estimated true score confidence intervals for the PASS and Full Scale standard scores are included in the Scale Norms conversion tables in Appendix B of the *CAS Administration and Scoring Manual*.

version system, this table provides the standard score, percentile, and confidence intervals (90% and 95%) for all possible raw scores. (See Rapid Reference at left.)

CONCLUSIONS

Although this discussion of the scoring procedures for the CAS is comprehensive and thorough, practitioners may wish to consult the *Cognitive Assessment System Administration and Scoring Manual* for additional details. The procedures can be accomplished with minimal difficulty.

🦅 TEST YOURSELF 🦅

Fill out a CAS Record Form by using the following information. Take the raw scores and compute the subtest scaled scores as well as PASS and Full Scale standard scores. (Page references relate to the CAS Record Form.)

Chronological Age = 12 years 9 months 4 days

1. Matching Numbers

Item	Time in Seconds	Accuracy Score (Number Correct)	Ratio Score (see pp. 14–16), Ages 8–17
2	30	8	
3	78	7	
4	130	8	

2. Planned Codes

Item	Time in Seconds	Accuracy Score (Number Correct)	Ratio Score (see pp. 14–16), Ages 8–17
1	61	38	
2	61	37	

3. Planned Connections

Item	Time in Seconds
4	8
5	23
6	36
7	23
8	48

4. Nonverbal Matrices: Total number correct = 20

5. Verbal-Spatial Relations: Total number correct = 26

6. Figure Memory: Total number correct = 25

7. Expressive Attention

Item	Time in Seconds	Accuracy Score (Number Correct)
4	13	
5	25	
6	37	40

8. Number Detection

Item	Time in Seconds	Number Correct	Number of False Detections	Accuracy Score (Number Correct minus False Detections)
1	55	43	0	
2	141	30	1	

9. Receptive Attention

Item	Time in Seconds	Number Correct	Number of False Detections	Accuracy Score (Number Correct minus False Detections)
1	86	50	1	
2	180	46	0	

10. Word Series: Total number correct = 15

continued

11. Sentence Repetition: Total number correct = 11

12. Sentence Questions: Total number correct = 16

Answers: See Figure 3.9.

CAS Subtests	Raw Scores	Scaled Scores (Appendix A)				
Matching Numbers	16	12				
Planned Codes	74	10				
Planned Connections	138	11				
Nonverbal Matrices	20		11			
Verbal-Spatial Relations	26		18			
Figure Memory	25		18			
Expressive Attention	68			13		
Number Detection	62			11		
Receptive Attention	58			13		
Word Series	15				13	
Sentence Repetition	11				12	
Speech Rate/ Sentence Questions	16				13	
Sum of Subtest Scaled Scores		33	47	37	38	155
		PLAN	SIM	ATT	SUC	FS
PASS Scale Standard Scores (Appendix B)		106	136	115	115	123
Percentile Rank (Appendix B)		66	99.2	84	84	94
90 % Confidence Intervals (Appendix B) — Lower		113	140	121	120	127
Upper		98	127	106	107	117

Figure 3.9 Raw Scores, Scaled Scores, and Scale Standard Scores for the "Test Yourself" Illustration

Note. From Naglieri and Das (1997a).

Four

CAS INTERPRETATION

C AS interpretative methods should be applied flexibly and within the context of all available information about the child. PASS scores should be integrated with all other information so that a comprehensive view of the child can be obtained and, if appropriate, a thorough plan for intervention can be developed, implemented, and evaluated.

STEPS FOR INTERPRETING CAS RESULTS

Interpretation of CAS scores involves several procedures, including an examination of the PASS scales and subtest scores and a comparison of CAS results with those of other tests (measures of achievement, rating scales, etc.) or test-retest comparisons. In carrying out these procedures five steps may be followed, as described in the following sections. Page 2 of the CAS Record Form provides a convenient place to record the various scores involved in these interpretative steps.

Step 1—Describe the CAS Full Scale and PASS Scale Standard Scores

The first step in interpreting the CAS is to evaluate the child's overall levels of performance by describing the PASS and Full Scale standard scores using the categories provided in Table 4.1. Further description of the scores includes the confidence intervals and percentile ranks that are provided in the sum of scaled score to raw score conversion tables (see Table 4.2). Note that the table includes estimated true scores based on confidence intervals and percentile ranks based on the normal curve. All this information should be recorded on the front of the CAS Record Form.

Table 4.1 Descriptive Categories of PASS and Full Scale Standard Scores

| Standard scores | Classification | Percent Included | |
		Theoretical normal curve	Standardization sample
130 and above	Very Superior	2.2%	1.8%
120–129	Superior	6.7%	7.8%
110–119	High Average	16.1%	17.6%
90–109	Average	50.0%	49.0%
80–89	Low Average	16.1%	14.5%
70–79	Below Average	6.7%	6.8%
59 and below	Well Below Average	2.2%	2.5%

Note. The percentages shown are for the Full Scale and are based on the total standardization sample ($N = 2,200$). From Naglieri & Das, 1997c.

CAS Standard Scores

The CAS Full Scale, Planning, Attention, Simultaneous, and Successive Scale standard scores are set at a mean of 100 and standard deviation of 15 based on a large and representative standardization sample (see Rapid Reference on page 72). The Full Scale score is an overall estimate of cognitive processing based on the combination of all the subtest scores included in the four PASS areas. It is a good general description of a child's cognitive processing when the four PASS Scale scores are similar. However, when there is significant variation among the PASS Scale standard scores, emphasis on the Full Scale score may obscure important relative strengths and weaknesses (this will be discussed later in the chapter). When this happens, the Full Scale score should be clarified (as a midpoint between extreme scores) or de-emphasized.

Descriptive Categories

The descriptive categories corresponding to standard scores, provided in Table 4.1, are used when a simple explanation is needed of the child's Full Scale and PASS Scale standard score performance. These categories qualita-

Table 4.2 Example of Standard Score Conversion Table for CAS

Sum of 12 Scaled Scores	Standard Score	Percentile Rank	Confidence Interval 90%	95%	Sum of 12 Scaled Scores
121	101	53	96–106	95–107	165
122	101	53	96–106	95–107	166
123	102	55	97–107	96–108	167
124	103	58	98–108	97–109	168
125	103	58	98–108	97–109	169
126	104	61	99–109	98–110	170
127	105	63	100–110	99–111	171
128	105	63	100–110	99–111	172
129	106	66	101–111	100–112	173
130	106	66	101–111	100–112	174
131	107	68	102–112	101–112	175
132	107	68	102–112	101–112	176
133	108	70	103–113	102–113	177
134	109	73	104–113	103–114	178
135	109	73	104–113	103–114	179
136	110	75	105–114	104–115	180

Note. From Naglieri & Das, 1997c.

tively summarize the child's scores but are not intended to be diagnostic. The advantage of such a classification system is that it provides a means of describing the standard scores in an understandable, not-too-technical manner.

CAS Percentile Ranks

The PASS and Full Scale standard scores that are associated with normal curve percentile ranks are provided in the respective norms conversion tables (see Table 4.2). These scores can be interpreted as a ranking of a child's per-

≡ Rapid Reference

The CAS standardization sample was stratified on the following variables:
- Age (5 years 0 months through 17 years 11 months)
- Gender (female, male)
- Race (black, white, Asian, Native American, other)
- Hispanic origin (Hispanic, non-Hispanic)
- Region (Midwest, Northeast, South, West)
- Community Setting (urban/suburban, rural)
- Classroom Placement (full-time regular classroom, part-time special education resource, full-time self-contained special education)
- Educational Classification (learning disability, speech/language impairment, social-emotional disability, mental retardation, giftedness, non-special education)
- Parental Educational Attainment Level (less than high school degree, high school graduate or equivalent, some college or technical school, 4 or more years of college)

formance relative to the rankings of children of comparable age in the standardization group. Thus a percentile rank of 16 can be interpreted as indicating that the child's score on a particular measure is equal to or greater than 16% of the scores obtained by the child's peer group in the standardization sample. In other words, the child scored as well or better than 16% of the children in the normative sample.

CAS Confidence Intervals

Confidence intervals are derived directly from the test's reliability coefficients (see Rapid Reference on page 73). They offer a way to estimate the precision of test scores and provide a range of values within which the child's true score is likely to fall. Estimated true score–based confidence intervals are provided in the PASS and Full Scale standard score conversion tables (Appendix B of the *Cognitive Assessment System Administration and*

DON'T FORGET

The PASS Scale yields standard scores that are set at a mean of 100 and standard deviation of 15. The CAS subtests yield scaled scores set at a mean of 10 and standard deviation of 3.

Scoring Manual [Naglieri & Das, 1997b]) for all possible values (see Table 4.2), making calculation unnecessary. The range of scores that represent the 90% and 95% levels of confidence around the estimated true scores are given. The 90% level of confidence is recommended for most purposes. This describes the range within which a child's true scores are found 90% of the time.

≡ *Rapid Reference*

CAS Reliability Coefficients

	Standard	Basic
Planning	.88	.85
Simultaneous	.93	.90
Attention	.88	.84
Successive	.93	.90
Full Scale	.96	.87

Step 2—Compare the Four PASS Standard Scores

One of the main purposes of the CAS is to examine variability across PASS scores to determine if the child has cognitive strengths or weaknesses. There are two factors to consider when PASS variation is examined: (a) the statistical significance of the profile of scores, and (b) the percentages of children in the standardization sample with such differences. The statistical significance of the variation in PASS scores—that is, the profile—is evaluated by using an intraindividual or ipsative (Kaufman, 1994) method. These procedures help distinguish between (a) differences that are related to error associated with reliability of the scales, and (b) differences that occur when the PASS variation can be interpreted within the context of the theory, related to strategy use, and evaluated in relation to achievement tests.

PASS cognitive processing strengths (scores that are significantly greater than the child's mean score) or weaknesses (scores that are significantly lower than the child's mean score) are found if a score is significantly high or low relative to the child's average level of performance. Because the PASS scores are compared to the child's

DON'T FORGET

One of the main goals of the CAS is to illuminate the connection between PASS theory and application of the theory to test interpretation. The emphasis therefore is on the four PASS scales because they reflect the theory.

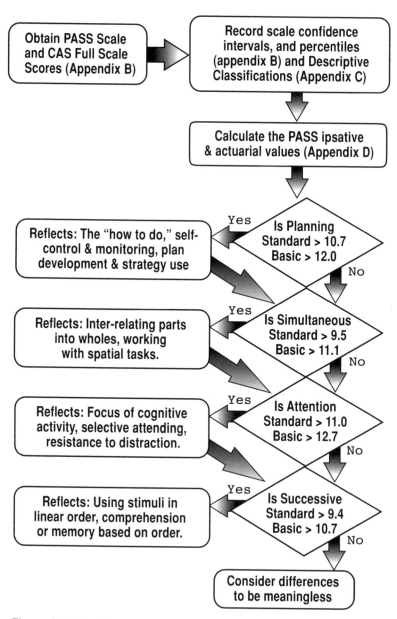

Figure 4.1 Flow Chart to Examine Overall CAS Scores and Compare the Four PASS Scales

Note. Appendices cited in flow chart are from Naglieri and Das (1997b).

average (and not the normative mean of 100), this tells about the child's "relative" strengths or weaknesses. This approach has been used in intelligence testing (see Kaufman, 1994; Naglieri, 1993; Sattler, 1988) for some time and is illustrated in flow chart form in Figure 4.1.

The steps needed to determine if a child's PASS profile is significant are listed below and are illustrated with PASS scores presented in Figure 4.2. The values needed at different levels of significance for the Standard and Basic Batteries are shown in Table 4.3.

1. Calculate the average of the four PASS standard scores (see Figure 4.2).
2. Subtract the mean from each of the PASS standard scores to obtain the intraindividual difference scores.
3. Compare the intraindividual difference scores (ignore the sign) to the values in Table 4.3. When the difference score is equal to or greater than the tabled values, the score differs significantly from the child's average PASS Scale standard score.
4. Label any significant score that is above the mean as a strength and any that is below the mean as a weakness.
5. Any variation from the mean that is not significant should be considered chance fluctuation.

Illustration of the Intraindividual Method

Examination of the significance of the PASS profile is illustrated in Figure 4.2. In this example the PASS scores range from a low of 79 to a high of 103, with all but the Successive score falling within the Average range. In this example the Successive processing score is 15.3 standard score points lower than the child's mean of 94.3. When compared to the difference required for

CAS Worksheet

PASS Scale Comparisons
Compare each PASS Scale standard score to the child's mean PASS score using Tables D.1 and D.2 (Standard Battery) or D.3 and D.4 (Basic Battery).

	Standard Score	d value	circle .05 .10	% in sample
PLAN	101	6.8	S W (NS)	47
SIM	94	- 0.3	S W (NS)	100
ATT	103	8.8	S W (NS)	35
SUC	79	-15.3	(S) W NS	15
PASS mean	94.3			

Figure 4.2 Illustration of PASS Scale Score Comparisons

Note. From Naglieri and Das (1997a).

Table 4.3 Intraindividual Differences Needed for Significance Between Each PASS Score and the Child's Mean PASS Score for All Ages

	Standard Battery		Basic Battery	
	$p = .10$	$p = .05$	$p = .10$	$p = .05$
Planning	9.7	10.8	10.9	12.1
Simultaneous	8.6	9.6	10.0	11.2
Attention	9.9	11.1	11.5	12.8
Successive	8.6	9.5	9.7	10.8

Note. Data from Naglieri and Das (1997c) Tables D.1 and D.3. See those tables for the differences needed by age. The values for differences needed for significance were calculated at the .10 and .05 levels as suggested by Silverstein (1993) to obtain a balance of Type I and Type II errors.

significance at the p = .05 level (9.5) the Successive score can be said to be significantly lower than the child's mean. This indicates that the child's score represents a significant cognitive weakness.

DON'T FORGET

To compare the four PASS standard scores:

1. compute the average of the scores,
2. subtract the mean from each score to get the intraindividual difference score,
3. compare these values to those found in Table 4.3, and
4. determine if the PASS Scale scores show any strengths or weaknesses.

Cognitive and Relative Strengths and Weaknesses

When there are significant strengths and/or weaknesses in the PASS Scale profile, it is important to consider the child's level of performance in relation to the standardization sample. For example, if a child has a significant intraindividual difference score that also falls below a score of 90 (in the Low Average range or lower; see Figure 4.3), it should be labeled a *cognitive weakness*. This was the case in the illustration for intraindi-

Relative & Cognitive Weaknesses

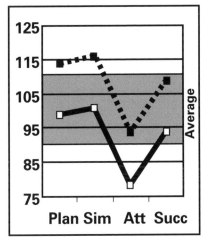

- **Relative Weakness**
  - significant weakness relative to the child's mean PASS score
- **Cognitive Weakness**
  - significant weakness relative to the child and
  - the PASS score falls below the Average range (less than 90)

Figure 4.3 Score Ranges Indicating Relative and Cognitive Weaknesses

vidual comparisons noted in Figure 4.2. In that example the Successive processing standard score is low relative to other PASS scores *and also* is below the Average category. Thus a dual criterion is used, on the basis of having a low PASS score relative to the child's mean and a low score relative to the norm group. In contrast, a child might have a significant weakness that still falls within the Average range (90 to 110); this score should be viewed as a *relative weakness* because it is low in relation to the child's mean but still within the average range of normative expectations. In this case the finding is important for different reasons (it might explain uneven performance for a child who typically functions very well) but is not the same as a cognitive weakness. A cognitive weakness is a more serious finding because it represents poor performance relative to peers as well as in comparison to the child's own average score.

Base Rates of Occurrence

PASS profiles can also be examined in relation to the frequency of occurrence of intraindividual differences in the standardization sample. This can be

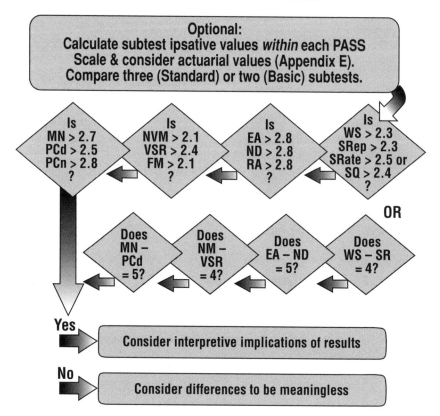

Figure 4.4 Flow Chart to Compare PASS Subtest Scores

determined through use of actuarial tables in Appendix D of the *Cognitive Assessment System Administration and Scoring Manual.* These tables give the frequency of occurrence of all possible intraindividual difference scores in the standardization sample. This can help determine how common or rare the PASS profile is and can therefore be helpful in establishing whether a pattern is typical or unusual. For example, according to the data provided in Figure 4.2, the difference of 15.3 found for the Successive Scale is significant from an intraindividual perspective and unusual (see Table 4.5) because a difference of that size occurred in only approximately 15% of the CAS standardization sample. The importance of this finding is augmented by the fact that a weakness of this size is uncommon among those in the normative group.

Two tables provided in this text give information about the base rates of

Table 4.4 Means and Standard Deviations (SDs) of Differences Between Each PASS Score and the Child's Mean PASS Score in CAS Standardization Sample for All Ages

	Standard Battery		Basic Battery	
	Mean	*SD*	*Mean*	*SD*
Planning	7.1	5.5	8.0	6.2
Simultaneous	7.4	5.7	7.7	5.9
Attention	7.3	5.5	7.8	6.0
Successive	8.5	6.3	8.7	6.7

Note. Data from Naglieri and Das (1997c) Tables D.2 and D.4. See those tables for the cumulative values for various percentages of the standardization sample.

PASS differences. Table 4.4 provides the means and standard deviations of differences between each PASS score and the child's mean PASS score for the entire standardization sample. The data show that on average children have about a 7-point (Standard Battery) or 8-point (Basic Battery) intraindividual difference. However, about a 10-point difference is needed for significance (see Table 4.3).

Table 4.5 shows the amount of intraindividual differences between each child's PASS scores and personal mean score found in 5% and 15% of the standardization sample. These values are useful for determining if a child's PASS profile is unusual. Those that are significant and unusual should be duly noted. Importantly, all cognitive weaknesses (see page 76) are unusual. The cognitive weaknesses in one of the PASS Scales are as follows: Planning = 7.6, Simultaneous = 5.7, Attention = 6.7, and Successive = 7.2.

Pairwise Comparisons of PASS Scales

When it is necessary to compare the difference between any pair of the four PASS scores, a simple pairwise comparison method can be used. Compare the difference between the pair of scores of interest to values required for significance that are summarized in Table 4.6. Values required when making these comparisons are provided in the *Cognitive Assessment System Administration*

Table 4.5 Selected Percentages of Standardization Sample with Differences Between Each PASS Score and the Child's Mean PASS Score

	Standard Battery		Basic Battery	
	15%	5%	15%	5%
Planning	13	18	15	20
Simultaneous	13	18	14	19
Attention	13	18	14	19
Successive	15	21	15	22

Note. Data from Naglieri and Das (1997c) Tables D.2 and D.4. See those tables for the cumulative values for various percentages of the standardization sample.

and Scoring Manual, Appendix D, for both the Standard and Basic Batteries. In addition, the frequency of occurrence (i.e., the extent to which the children in the standardization sample evidenced differences of varying sizes) is provided.

Step 3—Compare Subtest Scores Within Each Scale for Meaningful Discrepancies

Variation in CAS subtests, set at a mean of 10 and standard deviation of 3, can be examined by using the same method applied in studying the PASS profile. The subtest scaled scores are compared to the child's mean subtest score, and the presence of significant differences is determined. In addition, the frequency of occurrence of subtest differences is compared to that found for the normal standardization sample. These variations should also be interpreted within the context of the theory, consideration of strategy use, and other relevant variables (see Figure 4.4).

When to Do Subtest Analysis

The approaches described so far in this chapter are based on the assumption that the four theoretically derived PASS Scale scores will provide the most

Table 4.6 Pairwise Comparisons of PASS Scores Required for Significance at the .05 Level

	Plan	Sim	Att	Succ
Planning		13	14	13
Simultaneous	15		13	12
Attention	16	16		13
Successive	15	14	15	

Note. Differences for the Standard Battery appear above the diagonal and those for the Basic Battery appear below the diagonal. Data from Naglieri and Das (1997b) Table D.5.

important interpretive information. There may be instances, however, when the professional chooses to go further and examine the variation among the CAS subtest scores. Although this more detailed analysis has the advantage of facilitating a more specific examination of the child's performance, it has the disadvantage of involving scores with lower reliability than those of the PASS scales. Subtest-level analysis is therefore only considered when there is a specific reason to examine performance at this level.

Significant subtest score variation within a PASS scale can help determine if the entire scale or only one subtest from that scale had the most influence on the scale score. This provides a method to determine, for example, if a weakness in Planning is the result of poor performance on a single subtest or reflects consistently low scores. Subtest score analysis can also identify areas of relative weakness owing to the child's failure to use any strategy on one of the Planning subtests, in contrast to the other two subtests for which the child was able to devise a strategy. In such an instance it can be important to determine the significance of the difference among the child's scaled scores. See Table 4.7.

DON'T FORGET

The focus of CAS interpretation is at the PASS Scale level, *not* at the subtest level, because the test's theory guides the examination of a child's cognitive strengths and weaknesses.

Table 4.7 Values Needed to Compare Subtest Scores Within Each PASS Scale

	Differences required for significance		Percentages in standardization sample	
	$p = .10$	$p = .05$	15%	5%
Matching Numbers	2.5	2.8	2.2	3.3
Planned Codes	2.3	2.6	2.4	3.6
Planned Connections	2.5	2.9	2.3	3.3
Nonverbal Matrices	1.9	2.2	2.4	3.5
Verbal-Spatial Relations	2.2	2.5	2.7	3.8
Figure Memory	2.0	2.2	2.5	3.5
Expressive Attention	2.6	2.9	2.7	4.0
Number Detection	2.6	2.9	2.2	3.4
Receptive Attention	2.6	2.9	2.2	3.3
(ages 5–7)				
Word Series	2.2	2.4	2.5	3.4
Sentence Repetition	2.1	2.4	2.1	3.1
Speech Rate	2.3	2.6	2.7	3.9
(ages 8–17)				
Word Series	2.2	2.4	2.1	3.1
Sentence Repetition	2.1	2.4	1.7	2.5
Sentence Questions	2.2	2.5	2.0	2.9

Note. Data from Naglieri and Das (1997c) Tables E.1 and E.2. See those tables for values by age and the cumulative values for various percentages of the standardization sample.

Subtest Comparison Example

The intraindividual comparison of subtest performance within each PASS scale is illustrated in Figure 4.5. In the example the Planned Connections subtest score of 7 is 3.0 points below the Planning mean of 10.0. This exceeds the tabled value of 2.9 (refer to Table 4.7 for the $p = .05$ level), which allows the practitioner to interpret this score as a

Subtest Analysis

Compare each subtest scaled score to the child's mean subtest score using Tables E.1 and E.2.

	Scaled Score	d value	circle .05 .10	% in sample
MN	11	1.0	S W (NS)	>25
PCd	12	2.0	S W (NS)	> 25
PCn	7	-3.0	(S) W NS	<10
PLAN mean	10.0			

Figure 4.5 Comparison of Planning Subtest Scores

Note. From Naglieri and Das (1997a).

significant weakness relative to the mean of the Planning subtests. In addition, this difference is unusual (refer to Table 4.7 for the percentages in standardization sample) because a difference of this size occurred in less than 5% of the standardization sample.

Pairwise Comparisons of CAS Subtests

When the CAS Basic Battery is used, analysis of subtest performance within each PASS scale can only be done using a pairwise method. Compare the two subtests within each of scales by using the values in Table 4.8. Calculate the difference between the two subtests (ignore the sign) and compare the result to the tabled values. If the difference obtained is equal to or greater than that found in the table, then the two scores differ significantly. Actuarial values are also provided in Appendix E of the *Cognitive Assessment System Administration and Scoring Manual*. See Figure 4.4 for an illustration of the steps in this method.

Age Equivalents

Age-equivalent scores are provided in Appendix E of the *Cognitive Assessment System Administration and Scoring Manual*. These scores should be interpreted with considerable caution (see Sattler, 1988) and are of greatest value in explaining test results in a nontechnical way to parents.

Step 4—Compare the Full Scale and PASS Standard Scores With Achievement Scores

The CAS scores can be used to help determine if a child's achievement is below expectations and to assist when interventions are planned as well as when

Table 4.8 Values Needed to Make Pairwise Comparisons of Subtests Within Each PASS Scale

	Differences required for significance		Percentages in standardization sample	
	$p = .01$	$p = .05$	15%	5%
Matching Numbers with Planned Codes	5	4	4	6
Nonverbal Matrices with Verbal-Spatial Relations	4	3	4	6
Expressive Attention with Number Detection	5	4	4	6
Word Series with Sentence Repetition	4	3	3	5

Note. Data abstracted from Naglieri and Das (1997b) Tables E.3 and E.4. See those tables for more information.

eligibility for special education services is considered. There are two methods for comparing the CAS scores to achievement, both of which fit within a theoretical framework designed to discover if the child has a PASS cognitive weakness and an associated academic weakness. One method involves comparing CAS scores with achievement; the other involves applying a theoretical system for interpretation of these differences. The various steps of each method are illustrated in Figure 4.6.

The Simple Difference Approach

The values needed to compare CAS scores and performance on several achievement tests by using the simple difference method are provided in Table 4.9 for the Standard Battery and Table 4.10 for the Basic Battery. The differences between each of the PASS scores and the achievement test scores were computed for the .05 and .01 levels of significance by using the method described earlier for the PASS pairwise comparisons.

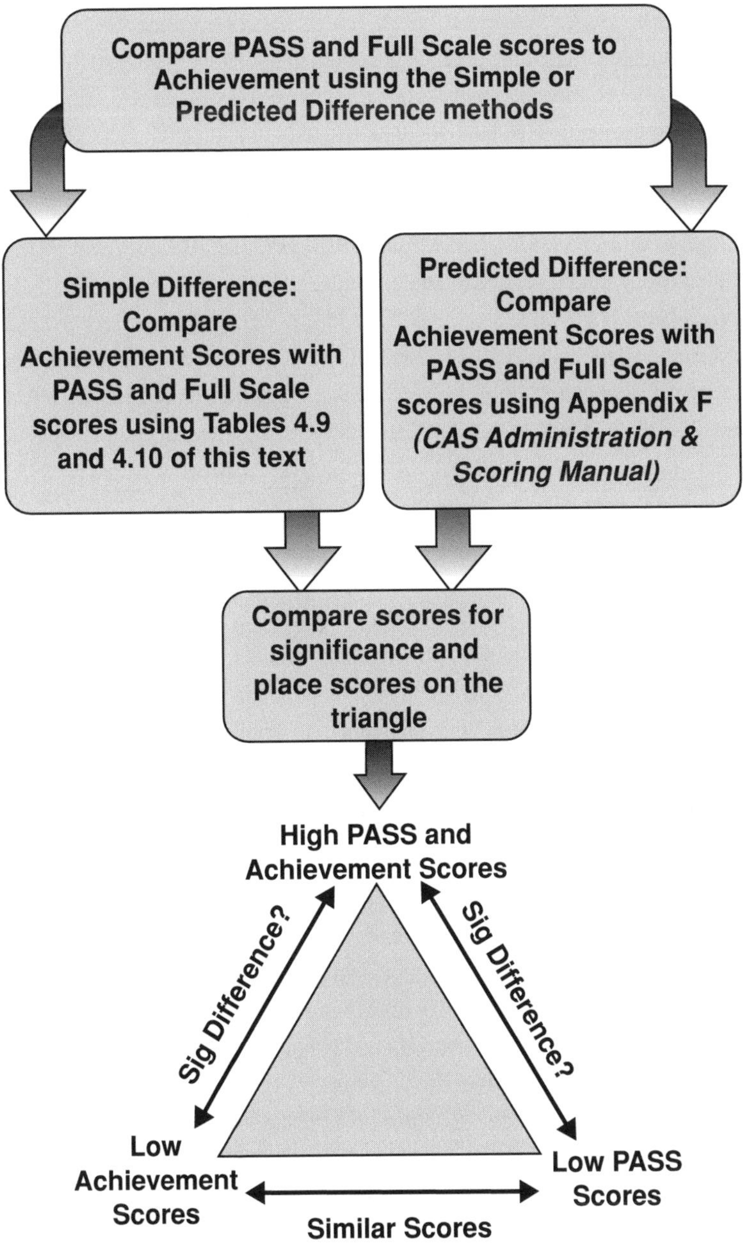

Compare PASS and Full Scale scores to Achievement using the Simple or Predicted Difference methods

Simple Difference: Compare Achievement Scores with PASS and Full Scale scores using Tables 4.9 and 4.10 of this text

Predicted Difference: Compare Achievement Scores with PASS and Full Scale scores using Appendix F *(CAS Administration & Scoring Manual)*

Compare scores for significance and place scores on the triangle

High PASS and Achievement Scores

Sig Difference?

Sig Difference?

Low Achievement Scores

Low PASS Scores

Similar Scores

Figure 4.6 Flow Chart to Compare PASS and Achievement Test Scores

The simple difference method provides values needed for significance when comparing PASS and Full Scale standard scores to those standard scores earned on any of several achievement tests. The formula used is the same one employed to compute similar comparisons (e.g., with the Wechsler Verbal and Performance Scales) and is described in Appendix C (pp. 155–158) of the *Cognitive Assessment System Interpretive Handbook* (Naglieri & Das, 1997c).

Values needed to apply the simple difference method are used in the following manner. First, compare the absolute value of the difference between the two scores to the tabled values. When the difference between the CAS and achievement scores is equal to or greater than the tabled value, the difference is significant. For example, if a child earns a CAS Full Scale standard score of 97 on the Standard Battery and a Kaufman Test of Educational Achievement (K-TEA; Kaufman & Kaufman, 1998) Reading Comprehension score of 87, the 10-point difference is significant at $p = .05$ (see Table 4.9).

Owing to the fact that the CAS and the achievement tests listed in Tables 4.9 and 4.10 were not administered to the same sample of children, the percentage of children who earned differences of varying sizes is not provided. These tables provide data on significance, not on the frequency of occurrence of the differences. Nevertheless, the tables allow direct and useful comparisons of CAS scores with scores on a variety of achievement tests.

CAS and the Ability/Achievement Discrepancy/Consistency: A New Method

The significance of a difference between PASS and achievement test scores can be used to determine if an ability achievement discrepancy is present. In many states in the United States this is an important factor in determining whether the child is eligible for special education services. Traditionally the discrepancy has indicated that the child's actual level of achievement is not consistent with the level predicted by the IQ score. Such a finding, however, does not shed light on whether there is a cognitive explanation for the child's poor academic performance. Assuming that the academic weakness is not the result of sensory limitations, lack of educational opportunity, and so forth, in this situation the child is identified as disabled partially on the basis of *not* finding any cognitive problem.

The CAS allows practitioners to determine if there is a cognitive explanation for an academic problem, as well as what has traditionally been termed

Table 4.9 Values Needed to Compare Scores on CAS Standard Battery and Selected Achievement Tests (Simple Difference Method)

		$p = .05$					$p = .01$				
		Plan	Sim	Att	Succ	FS	Plan	Sim	Att	Succ	FS
DAB-2	Listening	12	11	12	11	9	16	14	16	14	12
	Speaking	12	10	12	10	9	16	13	16	13	12
	Reading	11	9	11	9	8	15	12	15	12	10
	Writing	11	8	11	8	7	14	11	14	11	9
	Mathematics	13	11	13	11	10	17	15	17	15	13
	Spoken Language	12	10	12	10	8	15	13	15	13	11
	Written Language	11	8	11	8	7	14	11	14	11	9
	TOTAL	11	9	11	9	7	14	12	14	12	9
K-TEA	Reading Decoding	12	11	12	10	9	16	14	16	14	11
	Reading Comprehension	13	12	13	11	10	17	15	17	15	13
	Reading Composite	11	10	12	10	8	15	13	15	13	11
	Math Applications	13	12	13	12	10	17	16	18	16	14
	Math Computation	13	12	13	12	10	17	16	17	15	13
	Math Composite	12	11	12	10	9	16	14	16	14	11
	Spelling	12	11	13	11	9	16	15	17	14	12
	Battery Composite	11	9	11	9	7	14	12	15	12	10
PIAT-R	General Information	11	10	12	10	8	15	13	15	13	11
	Reading Recognition	11	9	11	9	7	14	12	15	12	10
	Reading Comprehension	11	10	12	10	8	15	13	16	13	11
	Total Reading	12	11	13	11	9	16	14	17	14	12

continued

Table 4.9 continued

				$p = .05$						$p = .01$		
		Plan	Sim	Att	Succ	FS		Plan	Sim	Att	Succ	FS
	Mathematics	11	10	11	9	8		15	13	15	12	10
	Spelling	11	10	11	9	8		15	13	15	12	10
	TOTAL TEST	15	14	15	14	13		20	19	20	18	17
WIAT	Basic Reading	13	11	13	11	10		17	15	17	15	13
	Mathematics Reasoning	14	12	14	12	11		19	16	19	16	15
	Spelling	14	12	14	12	11		18	16	18	16	14
	Reading Comprehension	14	13	14	13	12		19	17	19	17	15
	Numerical Operations	15	14	15	14	13		20	18	20	18	17
	Listening Comprehension	16	14	16	14	13		21	19	21	19	18
	Oral Expression	13	12	13	12	11		18	15	18	15	14
	Written Expression	16	15	16	15	14		22	20	22	20	19
	Reading	12	10	12	10	9		16	13	16	13	12
	Mathematics	13	11	13	11	10		17	15	17	15	13
	Language	14	12	14	12	11		18	16	18	16	14
	Writing	14	12	14	12	11		18	16	18	16	14
	Screener	12	10	12	10	8		15	13	15	13	11
	TOTAL	11	9	11	9	8		15	12	15	12	10
WJ-R	Broad Reading	12	10	12	10	9		16	14	16	14	12
	Basic Reading	12	10	12	10	8		16	13	16	13	11
	Reading Comprehension	12	10	12	10	9		16	14	16	14	12
	Broad Math	13	11	13	11	9		17	14	17	14	12

Table 4.9 continued

			$p = .05$				$p = .01$				
		Plan	Sim	Att	Succ	FS	Plan	Sim	Att	Succ	FS
	Basic Math	13	11	13	11	10	17	15	17	15	13
	Math Reasoning	14	12	14	12	11	18	16	18	16	15
	Writing Skills	12	10	12	10	9	16	14	16	14	12
	Skills Cluster	12	10	12	10	8	15	13	15	13	11
	Letter Word Identification	13	11	13	11	9	17	14	17	14	12
	Passage Comprehension	14	13	14	13	12	19	17	19	17	15
	Calculation	13	12	13	12	11	18	15	18	15	14
	Applied Problems	14	12	14	12	11	18	16	18	16	15
	Dictation	14	12	14	12	11	18	16	18	16	14
	Word Attack	14	12	14	12	11	18	16	18	16	14
	Reading Vocabulary	13	11	13	11	10	17	15	17	15	13
	Quantitative Concepts	15	14	15	14	13	20	18	20	18	17
	Proofing	14	12	14	12	11	18	16	18	16	14
WRAT-3	Reading	13	12	14	12	11	18	16	18	16	14
BLUE	Spelling	14	13	14	13	11	18	17	18	16	15
	Arithmetic	15	14	15	14	13	20	18	20	18	17
WRAT-3	Reading	14	12	14	12	11	18	16	18	16	15
TAN	Spelling	14	13	14	13	11	18	17	19	17	15
	Arithmetic	15	14	16	14	13	20	19	20	19	17

Table 4.10 Values Needed to Compare Scores on CAS Basic Battery and Selected Achievement Tests (Simple Difference Method)

		$p = .05$					$p = .01$				
		Plan	Sim	Att	Succ	FS	Plan	Sim	Att	Succ	FS
DAB-2	Listening	13	12	14	12	13	18	15	18	15	17
	Speaking	13	11	13	11	12	17	15	18	15	16
	Reading	12	11	13	11	12	16	14	17	14	15
	Writing	12	10	12	10	11	15	13	16	13	14
	Mathematics	14	12	14	12	13	19	16	19	16	18
	Spoken Language	13	11	13	11	12	17	14	17	14	16
	Written Language	12	10	12	10	11	15	13	16	13	14
	TOTAL	12	10	12	10	11	16	13	16	13	15
K-TEA	Reading Decoding	13	12	14	11	12	17	15	18	15	16
	Reading Comprehension	14	13	14	12	13	18	17	19	16	17
	Reading Composite	12	11	13	11	12	16	15	17	14	16
	Math Applications	14	13	15	13	14	18	17	19	17	18
	Math Computation	14	13	15	13	13	18	17	19	16	18
	Math Composite	13	12	14	11	12	17	15	18	15	16
	Spelling	13	12	14	12	13	18	16	19	16	17
	Battery Composite	12	11	13	10	11	16	14	17	13	15
PIAT-R	General Information	12	11	13	11	12	16	15	18	14	16
	Reading Recognition	12	11	13	10	11	16	14	17	14	15
	Reading Comprehension	13	11	13	11	12	16	15	18	14	16
	Total Reading	13	12	14	12	13	17	16	18	15	17

Table 4.10 continued

		$p = .05$					$p = .01$				
		Plan	**Sim**	**Att**	**Succ**	**FS**	**Plan**	**Sim**	**Att**	**Succ**	**FS**
	Mathematics	12	11	13	11	12	16	14	17	14	15
	Spelling	12	11	13	11	12	16	14	17	14	15
	TOTAL TEST	16	15	17	15	16	21	20	22	19	20
WIAT	Basic Reading	14	12	14	12	13	19	16	19	16	18
	Mathematics Reasoning	15	13	15	13	14	20	18	20	18	19
	Spelling	15	13	15	13	14	19	17	20	17	19
	Reading Comprehension	15	14	16	14	15	20	18	20	18	19
	Numerical Operations	16	15	16	15	16	21	19	22	19	20
	Listening Comprehension	17	15	17	15	16	22	20	22	20	21
	Oral Expression	14	13	15	13	14	19	17	19	17	18
	Written Expression	17	16	17	16	17	23	21	23	21	22
	Reading	13	11	13	11	12	17	15	18	15	16
	Mathematics	14	12	14	12	13	19	16	19	16	18
	Language	15	13	15	13	14	19	17	20	17	19
	Writing	15	13	15	13	14	19	17	20	17	19
	Screener	13	11	13	11	12	17	14	17	14	16
	TOTAL	12	11	13	11	12	16	14	17	14	15
WJ-R	Broad Reading	13	11	14	11	13	17	15	18	15	17
	Basic Reading	13	11	13	11	12	17	15	17	14	16
	Reading Comprehension	13	11	14	11	13	17	15	18	15	17

continued

Table 4.10 continued

		p = .05					p = .01				
		Plan	Sim	Att	Succ	FS	Plan	Sim	Att	Succ	FS
	Broad Math	14	12	14	12	13	18	16	18	15	17
	Basic Math	14	12	14	12	13	18	16	19	16	17
	Math Reasoning	15	13	15	13	14	20	18	20	17	19
	Writing Skills	13	12	14	11	13	18	15	18	15	17
	Skills Cluster	13	11	13	11	12	17	14	17	14	16
	Letter Word Identification	14	12	14	11	13	18	16	18	15	17
	Passage Comprehension	15	14	15	13	15	20	18	20	18	19
	Calculation	14	13	15	12	14	19	17	19	16	18
	Applied Problems	15	13	15	13	14	20	18	20	17	19
	Dictation	15	13	15	13	14	19	17	20	17	18
	Word Attack	14	13	15	13	14	19	17	19	17	18
	Reading Vocabulary	14	12	14	12	13	18	16	19	16	18
	Quantitative Concepts	16	15	17	15	16	21	20	22	19	21
	Proofing	15	13	15	13	14	19	17	20	17	18
WRAT-3 BLUE	Reading	14	13	15	13	14	19	17	20	17	18
	Spelling	15	14	15	13	14	19	18	20	18	19
	Arithmetic	16	15	17	15	15	21	20	22	19	20
WRAT-3 TAN	Reading	14	13	15	13	14	19	18	20	17	18
	Spelling	15	14	15	13	14	19	18	20	18	19
	Arithmetic	16	15	17	15	16	21	20	22	20	21

an *ability/achievement discrepancy*. When a child's Full Scale or separate PASS Scale standard scores are significantly higher than his or her achievement scores, the discrepancy is found. However, because a child's weakness in a specific area of achievement (e.g., Reading Decoding) might be related to a specific weakness in a PASS area (e.g., Successive processing), the *consistency* between these two scores (Successive and Reading Decoding) as well as a *discrepancy* between other CAS scales and achievement scores can be found. The consistency between Successive processing and Reading Decoding is indicated by a non-significant difference between the scores. This evidence contributes to the interpretation that for an individual child Successive processing and Reading Decoding are related, as suggested by Kirby and Williams (1991). Such a suggestion has intervention implications (see Chapter 7).

Discrepancy/Consistency Approach

To apply this method, compare each of the PASS and Full Scale scores to achievement. Analyzing the sample scores presented in Table 4.11, it is found that the child's Successive score is significantly lower than his or her PASS mean. Similarly, the child has a low achievement test score in Reading Decoding on the K-TEA. This score is significantly lower than the Planning, Simultaneous, and Attention scores, but not significantly lower than the Successive score. In this case there is a discrepancy between (a) Planning, Attention, and Simultaneous scales with Successive, and (b) Planning, Attention, and Simultaneous scales with achievement. The lack of a significant difference between Successive and Reading Decoding (a relationship anticipated from previous research summarized in, for example, Das, Naglieri, & Kirby, 1994) provides an explanation for the academic problem. Considering the strong relationships between word decoding and Successive processing (Das, Naglieri, & Kirby, 1994; Kirby & Williams, 1991), the connection is well warranted. This case is illustrated in Figure 4.7, which shows the triangular relationship among the variables. At the base of the triangle are the two areas of weakness, one in achievement (K-TEA Reading Decoding) and one in cognitive processing (Successive). At the top of the triangle are the areas of the child's high scores. When this relationship is found, the practitioner has an important perspective on the child. This child has a cognitive weakness and associated academic weakness that warrant intervention.

When the practitioner fails to find a weakness in one of the PASS

Table 4.11 Example of Discrepancy/Consistency Method for Comparing CAS Results to Achievement

	Child's score	Difference score	PASS difference	Achievement difference
Planning	101	6.8	ns	sig
Simultaneous	94	−0.3	ns	sig
Attention	103	8.8	ns	sig
Successive	79	−15.3	sig	ns
K-TEA				
Reading Decoding	72			

Note. ns = not significant; sig = significant.

processes, evidence for a cognitive processing explanation of the academic weakness is not apparent. In such a case it is appropriate to consider variables in the environment that may be responsible for the academic failure. These include quantity and quality of instruction, motivation of the child, and so on. This is when direct instruction of the academic area should be considered.

Predicted Difference Approach

The comparison of ability and achievement test scores based on a simple difference method, although widely used, has psychometric limitations. It does not account for regression effects, it overestimates the frequency of a discrepancy for children with above average ability scores, and it underestimates the frequency of a discrepancy for children with below average ability scores (Reynolds, 1990). These problems are addressed through the application of a predicted difference method. In order to develop the values needed to

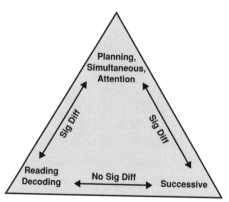

Figure 4.7 Relationship Among Variables (Sample Case)

use this method, however, both tests should be administered to the same sample and the relationships among the variables studied. Because the CAS and WJ-R (Woodcock-Johnson) achievement subtests were administered to a large, representative sample of students during standardization of

the CAS, a predicted difference method is possible. The values needed to compare the CAS PASS and Full Scale standard scores with WJ-R achievement test results are provided in the *Cognitive Assessment System Administration and Scoring Manual*, Appendix F. These tables are used to examine the discrepancy between an obtained achievement score and one that can be predicted from any PASS score.

The predicted difference method requires four steps. First, the achievement test score that is predicted from the CAS standard scores is obtained from the appropriate table. Second, the difference between the predicted and obtained achievement scores is calculated. Third, the difference between observed and predicted achievement scores is compared to tabled values to determine if a significant difference is found. Differences equal to or greater than the tabled values indicate that the obtained and predicted scores are discrepant. Fourth, the difference is compared to those found in the normative sample.

The predicted difference method is illustrated in Table 4.12. The obtained PASS and Full Scale scores are used to derive predicted Calculation scores by using Appendix F in the *Cognitive Assessment System Administration and Scoring Manual*. These scores are recorded in the Predicted Scores column of Table 4.12. The differences between each of the predicted scores and the obtained Calculation scores are recorded in the Difference Found column. The Differences Found are contrasted with the values needed for significance (Difference Needed column from Appendix F). Differences that are equal to or greater than the tabled values are significant. In this example, the Calculation scores predicted by the Planning Scale do not differ significantly (consistency), but the remaining CAS standard scores all differ from the Calculation score (discrepancy). Thus there is a significant difference between the Full

Table 4.12 Example of Predicted Difference Method for Comparing CAS Results to Achievement

	Obtained scores	Predicted scores	Difference needed	Difference found	sig/ns
Planning	77	87	15	16	ns
Simultaneous	94	97	25	17	sig
Attention	102	101	29	18	sig
Successive	102	101	29	19	sig
Full Scale	90	94	22	15	sig
Achievement test					
Calculation (WJ-R)	72				

Note. sig = significant; ns = not significant. Differences needed are at the .05 level.

Scale score and Calculation. In addition, the similarity in low scores obtained in both Planning and Calculation indicates that the cognitive weakness may be associated with the academic weakness.

Step 5—Comparison of CAS Scores Over Time

It is often important to administer a test of cognitive functioning on two occasions to monitor recovery or deterioration associated with neurological conditions, or to evaluate cognitive functioning that may have changed over the course of medical treatments. This may be especially important in evaluating the recovery of children who have experienced traumatic brain injury. The statistical significance of the differences between first and second Full Scale and PASS standard scores can be obtained by using a method described by Atkinson (1991). This involves comparison of the first test score with a range of scores that represents the variability expected by both regression to the mean and test reliability. The method can be applied when sufficient time has elapsed, for example, 6 to 12 months, so that minimal practice effects are anticipated.

The ranges of scores that are used to determine when significant change has occurred were calculated for the PASS and Full Scale standard scores for the Standard and Basic Batteries separately. The values appear in Appendix G of the *Cognitive Assessment System Administration and Scoring Manual*. Locate the table that corresponds to the CAS version given (Standard or Basic) and the PASS or Full Scale score. Next, find the initial test score in the left column and follow that row horizontally to obtain the range of scores. If the second test standard score falls outside of the range, it can be concluded that a significant difference was found between the initial and most recent scores. These values can be used to identify significant improvement in scores (first and second scores that increase over time) as well as significant deterioration (scores that decrease over time).

For example, consider a person who earns an initial Planning score of 72 (Standard Battery). According to Table G.2 of the manual, the range of Planning scores is 64 to 87. These values represent the amount of variation that would be expected if no reliable change is found. Any second test scores that are outside the range represent a significant change. If, however, the second test score falls inside the range found in the table, it can be concluded that any differences found reflect measurement error and regression effects. In this case any standard score above 87 indicates a significant improvement in Planning scores. Any score below 64 suggests significant deterioration.

When CAS scores are evaluated for changes over time, consider (a) the significance of the change, and (b) the relation of the second score to the normative mean. In the example for which the initial Planning Scale score is 72, if the second score is 94 the difference is significant and the second score is now within the average range (90 to 110). This could be described as an optimal outcome. If, however, the second score is 88, the difference is still significant (the second score is greater than 87), but the second score is well below the normative mean (19th percentile score that falls within the Low Average classification). The two criteria should be used to recognize both the significance of the change and the comparison of the child to the normative group. When both criteria are met, the child's degree of improvement can be considered optimal.

Communication of CAS Results

Description of the PASS processes in oral and written form requires an understanding of the theory and the nature of the four types of cognition (see

≡ Rapid Reference

How to describe Planning:

1. Developing and using strategies or plans to solve problems
2. Being able to demonstrate general organization of how a problem could be solved
3. Evaluating the environment to determine how a problem or task could be solved
4. Selecting and using information to solve a problem
5. Evaluating and selecting plans from one's personal base of knowledge
6. Making decisions about how to do things
7. Controlling behavior, impulses, and mental activity
8. Evaluating the effectiveness of plans or strategies
9. Selecting plans or strategies
10. Modifying plans or strategies to be more efficient
11. Effectively using information about how well the plan is working
12. Determining when the task has been competed appropriately
13. Exerting self-control and self-regulation
14. Defining a problem (need for a plan), selecting a plan, and applying a plan to solve a problem (completing a task)

How to describe Attention:

1. Focusing concentration on one activity
2. Resisting distractions
3. Making effortful focus of activity
4. Paying selective attention to one variable to the exclusion of others
5. Maintaining focus over time
6. Responding to stimuli from the environment

How to describe Simultaneous processing:

1. Relating parts into a comprehensive whole
2. Seeing how things fit together
3. Understanding relationships among words, figures, or ideas
4. Working with spatial relationships
5. Seeing several things at one time
6. Integrating words into larger ideas

How to describe Successive processing:

1. Working with things in a specific linear order
2. Ordering sounds or words in a prescribed manner
3. Comprehending ideas or information based on serial order
4. Perceiving stimuli presented in a sequence
5. Executing movements in a specific linear order
6. Remembering and holding sounds or words in sequences
7. Retaining sequences of events from text
8. Demonstrating serial organization of speech

Rapid Reference on page 98). Readers should refer to Chapter 1 of this text or sources cited in that chapter for more information on PASS or its foundation. In the following discussion, general descriptive terms for the four processes are suggested and illustrated in a case example.

Case Example

The case illustration involves a young girl named Susie who attends a school for children with learning disabilities. This is not an imaginary case but a real child—one of the subjects who participated in a math intervention study reported by Naglieri and Gottling (1997). Her name has been changed to protect her identity. Both CAS and actual results of the classroom intervention are provided in this example. Her actual CAS scores are found in Table 4.13, and what follows is a narrative presentation of her performance. The example illustrates how the CAS results could be described, but additional test results that might normally accompany the CAS and K-TEA scores are not included in this example. Thus the example is not intended to provide a complete case study with all other test data that usually accompany a full evaluation. Instead, the goal is to show how the PASS and Full Scale results might be described and then used to identify an appropriate instructional approach, and how the effectiveness of the intervention can be determined.

DON'T FORGET

Use the CAS interpretive flow charts found in Figures 4.1, 4.4, and 4.6 to guide you though the interpretation of PASS scores.

Table 4.13 Case Example of Susie

	Standard score	Percentile	90% Confidence interval range	Difference from mean	Difference needed	sig/ns
Planning	79	8	74–89	−12.0	10.8	sig
Simultaneous	89	23	83–96	−2.0	9.6	ns
Attention	98	45	91–106	7.0	11.0	ns
Successive	98	45	92–105	7.0	9.5	ns
PASS mean	91					
Full Scale	88	21	84–93			
K-TEA						
Math Applications	91					
Mathematics Computation	76					

Note. sig = significant; ns = not significant.

Test Results and Interpretation Susie earned a CAS Full Scale score of 88, which falls within the Low Average classification. Her Full Scale score is ranked at the 21st percentile, which is equal to or greater than 21% of the scores obtained by children her age who were included in the standardization group. There is a 90% probability that Susie's true Full Scale score falls within the range of 84 to 90; however, there was significant variation among the separate scales of the CAS. For example, her Planning score is classified as Below Average and her Simultaneous score is Low Average, but her Attention and Successive standard scores are within the Average range. Thus the Full Scale score is inconsistent with some of the PASS scores. It is important to note that Susie's Planning Scale score is significantly lower than the mean of the four PASS Scale scores, indicating that an important weakness has been detected.

Susie earned a significantly low score on measures of Planning processing, which indicates that she has a cognitive weakness. Her score of 79 on the Planning Scale (90% confidence interval is 74 to 89) reflects the difficulty she had in using efficient and effective strategies for problem solving. She had trouble making good decisions about how to complete several tests and failed to monitor the quality of her work. This resulted in poor completion of tasks owing to inadequate and inefficient solving methods. For example, on a test that required her to record a specific code that corresponded to four different letters, she did so in a disorganized way without following any apparent strategy. About 90% of children her age use strategies to solve these problems.

Susie's poor performance in Planning is especially important because it reveals a weakness both in relation to her overall PASS score and in relation to her peers' scores. The low Planning score suggests that Susie has a cognitive weakness and that she will have difficulty in activities that demand development and/or use of strategies to solve problems, make decisions about how to do things, control behavior, self-monitor, and self-correct. These activities are especially important in academic areas such as mathematics computation.

Susie earned a K-TEA Mathematics Computation score that is as low as her cognitive weakness in Planning. In fact, there is no significant difference between these scores. Although her Mathematics Computation score of 76 (5th percentile) is similar to her Planning score (79, 8th percentile), it is significantly lower than her Mathematics Applications score of 91 (27th percentile). Additionally, her Mathematics Computation score is significantly lower than her Simultaneous, Attention, and Successive scores (therefore an ability achievement discrepancy has been found). Further, the consistency between her low scores in Mathematics Computation and Planning processing are likely related (which can be assessed via examination of her responsiveness to intervention; this is described later in the illustration). In contrast were Susie's scores on the remaining portions of the CAS.

Susie's Attention was measured by subtests that required her to focus on specific features of test material and resist reacting to distracting parts of the tests. She was able to concentrate and resist distractions well enough to earn a score of 98 on the CAS Attention Scale, which ranks at the 45th percentile and falls within the Average classification (90% range is 91 to 106). Attention tests required her to respond only to specific stimuli (e.g., the number 1 when it appeared in an outline typeface) but not to distracting stimuli (e.g., when the number 1 appeared in a regular typeface). Susie's score in Attention indicates that she demonstrated typical performance in both identifying targets and avoiding responses to distracting stimuli.

She also earned an Average score of 98 on Successive processing, which ranks at the 45th percentile (90% true score interval is 92 to 105). Her Successive processing was measured by tests that required her to work with information in a specific linear order. For example, she had to remember the order of words spoken by the examiner and comprehend information based on the ordering of words.

Susie earned a score of 89 on Simultaneous processing, which ranks her at the 23rd percentile and falls at the juncture of Average and Low Average classifications. These tests required her to relate parts as a group or whole, understand relationships among words and diagrams, and work with spatial relationships. Her score on the Simultaneous Scale illustrates that she can solve problems that demand integration of information into groups at a level that is just about average.

In summary, Susie showed important variation among the four PASS scales. Although she earned scores that ranged from 89 to 98 on the Simultaneous, Successive, and Attention scales, she earned a score that showed cognitive weakness in Planning (79). This weakness in Planning is reflected in her similar score on the K-TEA Math Computation subtest; both measures demand careful control of activity, selection of appropriate strategies to complete the problems, and self-monitoring (checking one's work). These results indicate that interventions should be considered for Susie that address both the academic and Planning processing demands of these tasks.

Intervention Design In addressing the Planning component of Susie's math computation problems, an intervention described by Naglieri and Gottling (1997) was applied. The regular teacher, using math worksheets consistent with the teacher's instructional objectives and curriculum, gave the intervention to the entire class. The teacher taught in half-hour segments following the format of 10 minutes of math worksheet activity, 10 minutes of discussion, and 10 minutes of math worksheet. During the 10-minute discussion period the teacher facilitated an interaction designed to encourage the children to consider how they completed the work and how they would go about completing the pages in the future. The teacher did not attempt to reinforce or otherwise encourage the children to complete the math in any particular

≡ *Rapid Reference*

Teacher Probes

Tell me how you did the problems.

Did it work as you expected?

What did this teach you?

How will you complete the page next time?

What are some reasons why you made mistakes on these problems?

How can you make the problems easier and get more done?

What seemed to work well for you before?

Will you do anything differently next time?

manner. For example, if a child reported using a particular strategy, the teacher did not say "Good job" but instead encouraged all the children to think about how they had done the work and what methods were effective.

In general, the teacher encouraged Susie's class to describe how they did the worksheets and discuss their ideas and methods (this facilitates planning). In addition, the children were asked to explain why some methods worked better than others. The goal was to teach the children to be self-reflective and self-evaluative (see Rapid Reference above for teacher probes). The teacher's job in this intervention was to facilitate self-awareness and self-reflection through class interaction and not specifically instruct the children to use strategies (see Chapter 7 for more details).

Response to Intervention Susie reported that she developed and used several methods for completing the math pages. First, she found it very difficult to concentrate because she was sitting next to someone noisy and disruptive. She moved to a quieter part of the room so she could do her work and not be distracted. Second, she noticed that she needed to review basic math facts. She did so by making flash cards and working with one of her friends. Third, she reported that she used to do math problems quickly and without checking her work, often writing in a sloppy and messy manner. This caused errors—for example, when she added columns that were not aligned properly. Finally, Susie reported that she realized it was better to get the problems done correctly rather

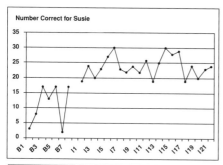

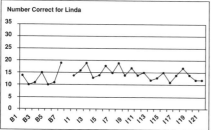

Figure 4.8 Comparison of Responses to Intervention (Susie and Linda)

Note. B = Baseline phase; I = Intervention phase.

than get as many finished as she could in the time allotted.

Susie's response to this intervention was compared to that of another student (Linda) who had similar scores in Simultaneous (90), Attention (85), and Successive (94) but a different score in Planning (106). The number of math problems each student got correct on each worksheet during baseline and intervention phases is shown in Figure 4.8. Susie improved considerably from baseline to intervention, more than doubling the number of problems correct per worksheet. In contrast, Linda performed at about the same level during baseline and intervention.

Evaluation of Intervention Success Susie's response to intervention suggests that improvement was being made with a cognitively based instructional method. The longer-term effectiveness of continued treatment like that described above, as well as more academically focused interventions, should also be determined. The effects of treatment could be evaluated by using the pre-post method described earlier. Recall that this method provides a way to test the significance of the differences between pre- and post-treatment scores on a standardized test. In this case the initial K-TEA score of 76 is compared to a range of test scores that would be expected on the basis of regression to the mean and reliability. Susie's initial Math Computation score (assuming a reliability of .93) of 76 has a range of scores (69 to 87) that are expected on the basis of reliability and regression to the mean. To obtain this value from Table 4.14, look in the column labeled .93 (the reliability of the Math Computation score) and read down the row that corresponds to the first test score until you find 76. Reading across the table, the range 69 to 87 is found. If Susie's score on Math Computation after academic instruction is less than

Table 4.14 Score Ranges Used to Determine Significant Change in Achievement Test Scores Over Time

First score	.99 Second score range	.98 Second score range	.97 Second score range	.96 Second score range	.95 Second score range	.94 Second score range
90	87–94	85–95	84–96	84–97	83–98	82–99
89	86–93	84–94	83–95	83–96	82–97	81–98
88	85–92	83–93	82–94	82–95	81–96	80–97
87	84–91	82–92	81–93	81–94	80–95	79–96
86	83–90	81–91	80–92	80–93	79–94	78–95
85	82–89	80–90	79–91	79–92	78–93	78–94
84	81–88	79–89	78–90	78–92	77–92	77–93
83	80–87	78–88	78–89	77–91	76–92	76–92
82	79–86	77–87	77–89	76–90	75–91	75–91
81	78–85	76–86	76–88	75–89	74–90	74–91
80	77–84	76–85	75–87	74–88	73–89	73–90
79	76–83	75–84	74–86	73–87	72–88	72–89
78	75–82	74–83	73–85	72–86	71–87	71–88
77	74–81	73–82	72–84	71–85	70–86	70–87
76	73–80	72–81	71–83	70–84	70–85	69–86

continued

Table 4.14 continued

First score	.99 Second score range	.98 Second score range	.97 Second score range	.96 Second score range	.95 Second score range	.94 Second score range
75	72–79	71–80	70–82	69–83	69–84	68–85
74	71–78	70–79	69–81	68–82	68–83	67–84
73	70–77	69–78	68–80	67–81	67–82	66–83
72	69–76	68–77	67–79	66–80	66–81	65–82
71	68–75	67–76	66–78	65–79	65–80	64–81
70	67–74	66–75	65–77	64–78	64–79	63–80
69	66–73	65–75	64–76	63–77	63–78	62–79
68	65–72	64–74	63–75	62–76	62–77	62–78
67	64–71	63–73	62–74	61–75	61–76	61–77
66	63–70	62–72	61–73	60–74	60–75	60–76
65	62–69	61–71	60–72	60–73	59–74	59–75
64	61–68	60–70	59–71	59–72	58–73	58–75
63	60–67	59–69	58–70	58–71	57–73	57–74
62	59–66	58–68	57–69	57–70	56–72	56–73
61	58–65	57–67	56–68	56–69	55–71	55–72
60	57–64	56–66	55–67	55–68	54–70	54–71

Table 4.14 continued

First score	.99 Second score range	.98 Second score range	.97 Second score range	.96 Second score range	.95 Second score range	.94 Second score range
59	56–63	55–65	54–66	54–68	53–69	53–70
58	55–62	54–64	53–65	53–67	52–68	52–69
57	54–61	53–63	52–64	52–66	51–67	51–68
56	53–60	52–62	51–63	51–65	51–66	50–67
55	52–59	51–61	50–62	50–64	50–65	49–66
54	51–58	50–60	49–61	49–63	49–64	48–65
53	50–57	49–59	48–60	48–62	48–63	47–64
52	49–56	48–58	47–59	47–61	47–62	46–63
51	48–55	47–57	46–58	46–60	46–61	46–62
50	47–54	46–56	46–57	45–59	45–60	45–61
49	46–53	45–55	45–57	44–58	44–59	44–60
48	45–52	44–54	44–56	43–57	43–58	43–60
47	44–51	43–53	43–55	42–56	42–57	42–59
46	43–50	42–52	42–54	41–55	41–56	41–58
45	42–49	41–51	41–53	40–54	40–55	40–57

continued

Table 4.14 continued

First score	.93 Second score range	.92 Second score range	.91 Second score range	.90 Second score range	.89 Second score range	.88 Second score range
90	82–100	81–100	81–101	80–102	80–102	80–103
89	81–99	80–100	80–100	79–101	79–101	79–102
88	80–98	79–99	79–99	78–100	78–101	78–101
87	79–97	78–98	78–98	78–99	77–100	77–100
86	78–96	77–97	77–97	77–98	76–99	76–99
85	77–95	77–96	76–97	76–97	75–98	75–98
84	76–94	76–95	75–96	75–96	75–97	74–98
83	75–93	75–94	74–95	74–95	74–96	73–97
82	74–92	74–93	73–94	73–95	73–95	72–96
81	73–91	73–92	73–93	72–94	72–94	72–95
80	72–90	72–91	72–92	71–93	71–93	71–94
79	71–90	71–90	71–91	70–92	70–93	70–93
78	70–89	70–89	70–90	69–91	69–92	69–92
77	70–88	69–88	69–89	69–90	68–91	68–91
76	69–87	68–88	68–88	68–89	67–90	67–91
75	68–86	67–87	67–87	67–88	67–89	66–90

Table 4.14 continued

First score	.93 Second score range	.92 Second score range	.91 Second score range	.90 Second score range	.89 Second score range	.88 Second score range
74	67–85	66–86	66–87	66–87	66–88	65–89
73	66–84	66–85	65–86	65–86	65–87	65–88
72	65–83	65–84	64–85	64–86	64–86	64–87
71	64–82	64–83	63–84	63–85	63–85	63–86
70	63–81	63–82	63–83	62–84	62–85	62–85
69	62–80	62–81	62–82	61–83	61–84	61–84
68	61–79	61–80	61–81	60–82	60–83	60–84
67	60–78	60–79	60–80	60–81	59–82	59–83
66	59–77	59–78	59–79	59–80	59–81	58–82
65	58–76	58–77	58–78	58–79	58–80	58–81
64	57–76	57–77	57–77	57–78	57–79	57–80
63	57–75	56–76	56–77	56–77	56–78	56–79
62	56–74	55–75	55–76	55–77	55–77	55–78
61	55–73	54–74	54–75	54–76	54–77	54–77

continued

Table 4.14 continued

First score	.93 Second score range	.92 Second score range	.91 Second score range	.90 Second score range	.89 Second score range	.88 Second score range
60	54–72	54–73	53–74	53–75	53–76	53–76
59	53–71	53–72	52–73	52–74	52–75	52–76
58	52–70	52–71	52–72	51–73	51–74	51–75
57	51–69	51–70	51–71	51–72	51–73	50–74
56	50–68	50–69	50–70	50–71	50–72	50–73
55	49–67	49–68	49–69	49–70	49–71	49–72
54	48–66	48–67	48–68	48–69	48–70	48–71
53	47–65	47–66	47–67	47–68	47–69	47–70
52	46–64	46–65	46–67	46–68	46–68	46–69
51	45–63	45–65	45–66	45–67	45–68	45–69
50	44–63	44–64	44–65	44–66	44–67	44–68
49	44–62	43–63	43–64	43–65	43–66	43–67
48	43–61	43–62	42–63	42–64	43–65	43–66

Table 4.14 continued

First score	.93 Second score range	.92 Second score range	.91 Second score range	.90 Second score range	.89 Second score range	.88 Second score range
47	42–60	42–61	42–62	42–63	42–64	42–65
46	41–59	41–60	41–61	41–62	41–63	41–64
45	40–58	40–59	40–60	40–61	40–62	40–63

87, then no significant improvement has been made. If, however, Susie's post-intervention score is above 87, then significant improvement has been found and the intervention can be viewed as effective. If Susie's post-intervention score is at least within the average range (90 to 110), the effects of intervention can be viewed as optimal.

CONCLUSIONS

This chapter provided a step-by-step explanation of how the CAS can be interpreted and used to assess changes in PASS processing over time as well as to evaluate the effectiveness of educational intervention. Significant variation in PASS processes may have relevance to instruction and methods that could be applied to evaluate the effectiveness of intervention. Evaluation of intervention success, illustrated in the case study, involved the collection of daily performance data. To evaluate the effectiveness of the entire approach to treatment, a psychometrically rigorous method designed to assess the reliability of standardized test score changes was suggested. These two approaches provide a thorough system of evaluating children's response to educational intervention. In combination with information about a child's PASS cognitive profile, these methods can be used to apply the approaches described in Chapter 7, Making the Connection Between PASS and Intervention.

TEST YOURSELF

1. The focus of CAS interpretation is
   (a) at the subtest level.
   (b) at the Full Scale level.
   (c) at the Item level.
   (d) at the PASS Scale level.

2. A child with a Cognitive Weakness has
   (a) a significant PASS profile.
   (b) a significantly low subtest score.
   (c) a weakness in PASS that is <90.
   (d) all of the above.

3. Using the Standard Error of Prediction to evaluate pre-post-test changes takes into account

(a) the child's mean PASS score.

(b) regression to the mean.

(c) reliability of the separate PASS scales.

(d) b and c above.

4. Confidence intervals for **PASS** scales are

(a) based on the Estimate True score method.

(b) based on the Obtained score method.

(c) based on the Standard Error of Prediction (SEP).

(d) based on both a and b above.

5. Evaluation of treatment effectiveness should include comparison of

(a) performance on classroom tasks during baseline and intervention periods.

(b) pre- and post-test intervention scores on CAS.

(c) pre- and post-intervention scores on standardized achievement tests.

(d) a and c above.

Answers: 1. d; 2. c; 3. d; 4. a; 5. d

Five

STRENGTHS AND WEAKNESSES OF THE CAS

everal reviews of PASS theory and the CAS have appeared in journals and books. A discussion of these reviews (both positive and critical) and research that is relevant to the issues they raise will enable the reader to assess the reviewers' comments and the research base that relates to, or clarifies, them.

SUMMARY OF REVIEWS

In the book *Psychological Testing*, Anastasi and Urbina (1997) write that the Cognitive Assessment System "will become an important, as well as innovative, tool for the assessment of cognitive status . . . [which] . . . because of its sound theoretical and empirical bases and the careful, large-scale standardization . . . has been eagerly anticipated by many test users" (p. 233). Others who have evaluated the test and the PASS theory share this positive perspective. Kotarsky and Mason (in press) state that the "CAS has the potential to be a widely used test which is easily administered and scored, and it should prove to be a useful instrument among clinical and educational professionals in determining special needs of children. It is an especially valuable addition to the existing cognitive assessment tools, particularly in its different style and its practical addition of its assessment to intervention model."

Gindis (1996) provides a review of the PASS theory and the CAS, relating it to the work of Luria and Vygotsky and the demands of professionals who evaluate children on a daily basis. His review encompasses both the theoretical and practical aspects of the theory and the test, respectively. Gindis concludes his review by stating:

Columbus discovered America thinking he had just found the new way to the Orient. Das, Naglieri, and Kirby are thinking they just "use more modern technology" to create a "better theory," "a more valid understanding," as they stated in the concluding chapter. . . . In fact, they probably created a revolutionary advance in the domain of cognitive assessment. . . . This book is a window to the future and all those interested in the perspectives of our science and profession should be familiar with its content. (p. 308)

Gindis recognizes that evaluation of children is an important aspect of the work of school psychologists and those who work to help understand children's successes and failures. Like some, he is frustrated with the stagnation in the field of IQ testing and the continued reliance on technology developed during the early part of the 1900s. He states:

Unfortunately, at the end of the century school psychologists (who, by now, may know a great deal about the "cognitive revolution"), routinely administer intelligence tests that were constructed almost 50 years ago and which have undergone only cosmetic changes. The time has come for us, school psychologists, to look for a more valid understanding of human cognitive competency than is currently offered by the IQ notion. We need more valid identification and measurement of the cognitive foundation for success or failure than is offered by the IQ concept. Such understanding can lead to creating truly effective methods of helping children to overcome their cognitive deficits and realize their mental potential. It is, indeed, the right time for the "Assessment of Cognitive Processes: The PASS theory of intelligence" to be published. (p. 305)

From a very practical perspective, Gindis describes the relationship of the PASS theory to educational problems. He describes the CAS as a comprehensive battery of tests that are "the most creative, clinically informative, and 'fun-to-perform' activities one can find in the professional arsenal of a school psychologist" (p. 307). This, in combination with "its strong grounding in the experimental research of the last two decades makes the PASS model one of the most comprehensive and substantiated conceptualizations in contemporary psychology" (p. 305). Thus Gindis states that the PASS theory and the

DON'T FORGET

Strengths of the CAS

- Is based on a well-researched theory of cognitive processing
- Is based on a modern view of ability
- Measures important specific abilities rather than just general ability
- Does not have subtests that require achievement (e.g., arithmetic subtests found in traditional IQ tests)
- Does not have subtests that require language knowledge (e.g., vocabulary subtests found in traditional IQ tests), thereby making it fair for many children
- Has a broad standardization sample
- Contains PASS Scales and Full Scale with excellent reliability
- Has flexible administration that allows the examiner to explain what is required in any language (e.g., Provide Help Guidelines)
- Has scales designed to measure planning and attention—something other tests do not have
- Is strongly predictive of achievement
- Shows different profiles for exceptional children such as ADHD and Reading Disabled
- Can uncover cognitive weaknesses related to academic failure that are consistent with the academic problems
- Can provide information about ability/achievement discrepancies and ability/achievement consistencies
- Is relevant to instruction and selection of specific interventions that match the child's cognitive characteristics

CAS stand out "as a landmark event in the field of educational/school psychology" (p. 305).

Another review is provided by Carroll (1995) and is discussed here in relation to Roodin's (1996) comments. Carroll approaches his review of the PASS theory (Das, Naglieri, & Kirby, 1994) from the perspective of factor analysis, and he raises two criticisms: (a) that sufficient factorial support for the PASS subtests was not found, and (b) that the Planning Scale could be better described as a measure of Perceptual Speed. These criticisms, especially the former, have been repeated, for example, by Flanagan, Andrews, and Genshaft (1997) with little consideration of the data available since the time of Carroll's review. There are two important points to consider when reading Carroll's review. First, his examination of the Das, Naglieri, and Kirby (1994) PASS book was limited by his overemphasis on factor analysis and his failure to consider other appropriate dimensions of validity that are amply presented in the text. Second, his conclusions were made on the basis of his re-factor analysis of research published using old versions of PASS experimental tasks, and therefore his comments have very limited, if any, generalizability to the Cognitive Assessment System. Moreover, his criticisms and concerns are inconsistent with important evidence reported since the publication of his review in 1995. Nevertheless many of his concerns are addressed here.

Carroll (1995) concludes that "Das, Naglieri, and Kirby have not yet arrived at a persuasive, interpretable model of intellectual abilities that is supported adequately by empirical data. They have concentrated a small number of tests that they claim define concepts derived from Luria's theories, but they have not demonstrated that these tests consistently measure these concepts, and only those concepts. They have made few attempts to examine relationships between their tests and tests that have been used in more than 50 years of research in cognitive abilities, nor have they considered adequately factor structure" (p. 408). Thus the issues are as follows:

1. Is PASS supported by empirical data?
2. Do the tests measure the PASS constructs and not others?
3. What is the relationship between traditional tests and PASS?
4. Does the PASS theory have factor analytic support?

Is PASS Supported by Empirical Data?

The question of empirical support for PASS as measured by tests developed up to the point of Carroll's (1995) review and the support for the work published after that must be considered separately. Carroll seems unaware that prior to 1995 there were several books that summarized the literature on the PASS theory and its initial conceptualization as an information-processing model. In addition, there were many research papers published by a number of authors specifically on simultaneous and successive processes, and a few on planning. This does not include the many volumes by Luria—"most frequently cited Soviet scholar in American, British, and Canadian psychology periodicals" (Solso & Hoffman, 1991, p. 251)—and those on which he based his work. For example, Das, Kirby, and Jarman (1979) summarized a number of important research studies on their initial work involving such topics such as how the processes relate to mental retardation, learning disabilities, achievement, the culturally disadvantaged, linguistic variables, and intervention. Similarly, Kirby's book *Cognitive Strategies and Educational Performance* (1984) discussed much research on planning as well as simultaneous and successive processes for children with learning and attention problems, and those with mental retardation; it also includes several chapters on cross-cultural studies. Similarly, Das, Naglieri, and Kirby (1994) summarized considerable experimental research on the PASS theory. Carroll apparently did not integrate the large amount of research support for various aspects of the PASS theory in his evaluation of the theory.

The amount of research support for the PASS theory described above is recognized by Roodin (1996) in his review. He describes the research on PASS theory as extensive and states that "the text provides empirical validation from many sources for each of the major points developed; this is a strength of the work" and that the theory "is firmly grounded in empirical data" (p. 342). Thus it appears that Carroll's perspective on the validity support for the PASS theory is different from that of Gindis and Roodin.

Do the Tests Measure the PASS Constructs and Not Others?

Carroll's second criticism centers on his reinterpretation of the CAS Planning subtests as measures of speed. It is unclear how he arrived at this position, especially because no evidence is provided to support his opinion. For example, he does not show that Planning subtests loaded with pure speed tests in an experimental study. Instead, he seems to have taken the simple descriptions of the tests we provided and determined that they are better described as speed. Interestingly, he states that Das, Naglieri, and Kirby did not demonstrate that the tests measure planning and only planning; but neither does he demonstrate that the CAS tests measure speed. Most important, however, is the fact that data show children *do* use strategies to solve the Planning subtests and that planning and speed tests do not function in the same way; hence the reinterpretation of the tests as measuring speed is inappropriate. The data are presented below.

Prior to examining Carroll's critique of the CAS Planning subtests as speed, it is important to define the concept of speed. According to Jensen (1980), "one can measure a speed factor in almost pure form only by divesting the timed task as completely as possible of any cognitive difficulty whatsoever" (p. 136). He gives an example of a speed test as one that requires a person to make as many Xs as possible in a fixed period. Thus the task is simple, involving nothing more than repeating the same act (making one letter) as fast as possible. Moreover, Jensen notes that such tests have quite low correlations with general intelligence. These characteristics are *not* consistent with the CAS Planning subtests.

The Planning subtests are not simple measures that are devoid of cognitive difficulty. Each test requires the child to carefully examine the demands of the task, determine an efficient method to solve the problems, and monitor the effectiveness of methods that are applied. The evidence that these tests are solved through the use of plans or strategies was amply shown by Naglieri and Das (1997c). They report that the great majority of children in the standardization sample reported and/or were observed using strategies to solve the Planning subtests.

Figure 5.1 shows the percentage of children in the standardization group organized by age who used strategies to solve the Planning subtests. The data show that approximately 75% of young children (below age 8) and more than 90% of children from ages 8 to 17 in the standardization sample used strategies to solve the Planning subtests. In addition, Naglieri and Das (1997c) show that the strategies are differentially related to success on the subtests. That is, some strategies are effective; others, or the lack of a strategy, lead to lower subtest scores. Clearly these subtests involve the generation, use, and monitoring of plans and cannot be described as simple tests of speed as suggested by Carroll (1995). Other evidence that planning involves more than speed is apparent when predictive validity (correlation of planning with achievement versus correlation of speed with achievement) is considered.

In comparing the CAS Planning subtests to measures of speed, two sources of information were used. First, the *Cognitive Assessment System Interpretive Handbook* (Naglieri & Das, 1997c) provides information about the relation-

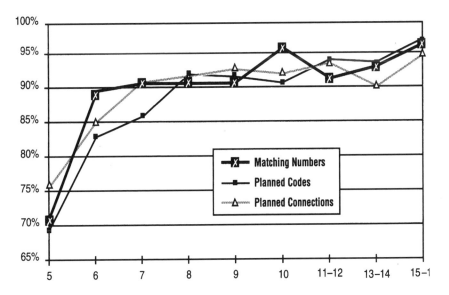

Figure 5.1 Percentages of Children (by Age) in CAS Standardization Sample That Used Strategies to Solve Planning Subtests.

Note. Data are from Naglieri and Das (1997c).

ships between PASS and achievement for a large, representative sample of children who were administered the CAS and the Woodcock-Johnson Revised Tests of Achievement during standardization of the instrument. That sample was organized into groups of children ages 5 to 7, 8 to 10, 11 to 13, and 14 to 17 (total $N = 1,600$). Then the Pearson correlations between Planning and Broad Mathematics and Mathematics Reasoning were computed. Next the data provided by McGrew and Hessler (1995) were used to obtain correlations between the WJ-R Cognitive Battery (Woodcock & Johnson, 1989b) Gs (Processing Speed) for the WJ-R standardization sample. This sample was also organized into groups of children ages 5 to 7, 8 to 10, 11 to 13, and 14 to 17. The correlations with speed as defined by Woodcock with both Broad Math and Mathematics Reasoning were found. The correlation coefficients were squared to determine the percentage of variance accounted for. Both the obtained correlations and amounts of variance are shown in Table 5.1.

The correlations and percentages of variance accounted for are informa-

Table 5.1 Correlations and Percentages of Variance Accounted for Between CAS Planning Scale and WJ-R Perceptual Speed Factor with Math Achievement

	Age group	CAS Planning		WJ-R Gs (Perceptual Speed)	
		Broad Math	Math Reasoning	Broad Math	Math Reasoning
Correlation	5–7	.53	.44	.37	.28
	8–10	.57	.51	.28	.22
	11–13	.60	.61	.20	.18
	14–17	.59	.53	.26	.18
Percentage of variance	5–7	28%	19%	14%	8%
	8–10	32%	26%	8%	5%
	11–13	36%	37%	4%	3%
	14–17	35%	28%	7%	3%

Note. CAS data are from Naglieri and Das (1997c) and WJ-R data are from McGrew and Hessler (1995).

tive. First, it is clear that Perceptual Speed accounts for considerably less variance than Planning and that the correlations decline across the age groups. In contrast, the correlations between Planning and Math show the increased importance of Planning with age. The evidence for the use of strategies on Planning tests, and the strong and consistent correlations between CAS and math achievement, do not support Carroll's re-interpretation of planning as speed.

What Is the Relationship Between Traditional Tests and PASS?

Das, Naglieri, and Kirby (1994) devote an entire chapter (Chapter 7) to the topic of how PASS relates to traditional IQ tests. In that chapter the PASS theory is related to the Wechsler scales, K-ABC, and the Stanford-Binet IV. It is suggested that these tests overlap with the Simultaneous and, to a limited extent, Successive portions of the PASS theory, but Planning and Attention are not measured. More important, however, the information provided in the *Cognitive Assessment System Interpretative Handbook* allows for comparison of the relative advantages and disadvantages of CAS and traditional IQ tests. Significant issues in this regard include (a) correlations to achievement, (b) relationships between CAS and the Wechsler scales, (c) profiles for exceptional children, and (d) relevance to intervention.

Correlations With Achievement

One of the most important dimensions of validity for a test of cognitive ability is the relationship to achievement (Brody, 1992; Cohen, Swerdlik, & Phillips, 1992). Whether one views intelligence as a general ability construct (e.g., the Wechsler or Stanford-Binet scales) or from a multidimensional perspective (PASS theory), the prediction of achievement offers an important way to evaluate the utility of the test's performance. If there is a strong relationship to achievement without content overlap, then whatever the test of ability measures can be said to include variables that are important for scholastic performance. Moreover, high correlations with achievement would also suggest explanatory power for exceptional children, something traditional IQ tests have had difficulty doing.

The relationship between PASS and achievement was one of the validity questions studied during final preparation of the CAS. This was especially important because only with large-scale studies can a good comparison be conducted of the relative strength of PASS in relation to traditional IQ tests. In order to cover this topic systematically, one must consider the context of what has been found for the Wechsler and Woodcock-Johnson, then the findings for the CAS. In each case it is important to emphasize large-scale studies of the relationships between achievement and ability.

Brody (1992) states that IQ typically correlates about .50 to .55, depending on age, with achievement. This statement is consistent with a study of the relationship between the WISC-III and Wechsler Individual Achievement Test (WIAT; Wechsler, 1992) conducted as part of the achievement test's standardization and validity efforts (see WIAT manual). A sample of 1,284 children ages 5 to 19 was administered both the WISC-III and WIAT. This sample included children from all regions of the country, representing different racial and ethnic groups, and with varying parental educational level. The correlations between the WISC-III FSIQ and WIAT subtests and

Table 5.2 Correlations Between WISC-III and WIAT

WISC-III	FSIQ	WISC-III	FSIQ
Basic Reading	.60	Written Expression	.46
Math Reasoning	.72	Reading	.68
Spelling	.52	Math	.71
Reading Comprehension	.67	Language	.58
Numerical Operations	.58	Writing	.53
Listening Comprehension	.61	Median	.59
Oral Expression	.42		

Note. $N = 1,284$ children ages 5 to 19. Data are from Wechsler's (1992) WIAT manual.

composites reported in Table C.1 of that manual range from .42 to .72 (median = .59) and are shown in Table 5.2.

A similar study of the relationship between ability and achievement was conducted by Elliott (1990). In the *Introductory and Technical Handbook* for the Differential Ability Scales (DAS), Tables 9.37 and 9.38, Elliott provides a study of the relationship between the DAS General Cognitive Ability (GCA) score with Basic Number Skills, Spelling, and Word Reading. This study involved a sample of 2,400 children included in the standardization sample for that test. The correlations between the total score on the DAS and achievement ranged from .52 to .60 (median = .60).

The relationship between the K-ABC Mental Processing Composite (MPC) with the K-ABC Achievement, Woodcock Reading Mastery Test, and KeyMath Diagnostic Math Test is reported by Kaufman and Kaufman (1983) in Tables 4.23 and 4.24 of their interpretative manual. In these studies of the predictive validity of the MPC, the correlations ranged from .47 to .74 (median = .63).

The relationship between the Woodcock-Johnson Cognitive and Achievement Test Batteries is provided in the *Woodcock-Johnson Technical Manual* (McGrew, Werder, & Woodcock, 1991) (Table H-3). This study involved several samples; of most interest to this discussion are the 6-, 9-, and 13-year-old groups. The median correlations across these ages between the WJ-R Broad

Table 5.3 Median Correlations Between WJ-R Broad Cognitive Ability and WJ-R Tests of Achievement

	WJ-R Broad Cognitive Ability		WJ-R Broad Cognitive Ability
Broad Reading	.67	Math Reasoning	.60
Basic Reading	.61	Basic Writing	.63
Reading Comprehension	.68	Skills Cluster	.71
Broad Math	.62	Median	.63
Basic Math	.61		

Note. $N = 888$; three age groups are represented (6, 9, and 13 years). Data are from McGrew, Werder, and Woodcock (1991).

Cognitive Ability Extended Battery and WJ-R Tests of Achievement were computed and are provided here in Table 5.3. The data show that the WJ-R correlations ranged from .61 to .71 (median = .63) with the WJ-R Tests of Achievement.

Finally, the correlation between the CAS Full Scale and the WJ-R Tests of Achievement is reported by Naglieri and Das (1997c; Table 4.16) for a representative sample of 1,600 children. This sample closely approximates the U.S. population on the basis of geographic region, parental education levels, race, ethnicity, and community setting. Table 5.4 provides the correlations between

Table 5.4 Median Correlations Between CAS FS and WJ-R Tests of Achievement

Broad Reading	.71	Math Reasoning	.67
Basic Reading	.68	Basic Writing	.66
Reading Comprehension	.72	Skills Cluster	.73
Broad Math	.72	Median	.70
Basic Math	.69		

Note. $N = 1,600$; children ages 5 to 17. Data are from Naglieri and Das (1997c).

Table 5.5 Summary of Predictive Validity of Selected Ability and Achievement Tests

	WISC-III FSIQ	DAS GCA	WJ-R Cognitive	K-ABC MPC	CAS FS
Median correlation	.590	.600	.625	.630	.700
Percentage of variance	35	36	39	40	49
Percentage increase over WISC-III	—	3	12	14	41
N	1,284	2,400	888	2,636	1,600

the CAS FS and the several achievement variables; the correlations range from .66 to .73 (median = .70) .

Table 5.5 provides a summary of the results of these large-scales studies of the relationship between measures of ability and achievement. The median correlation and the percentage of variance accounted for by these correlations is listed, along the with sample sizes. The data provide a comparison of the predictive validity of the various measures as presented by the respective authors in the test manuals. Although this comparison is limited by the fact that different achievement tests are used and different samples are involved, the samples are all large, in some cases representative of the U.S. population (WISC-III, DAS, and CAS). In addition, these studies do provide a means of comparing the relative power of the several tests of ability in the very important validity issue of prediction of achievement. The results suggest that of the possible options, the CAS FS score is the most powerful predictor of achievement. The results also contradict (a) Carroll's (1995) assertions that the PASS theory has limited empirical support, and (b) statements by McGrew, Keith, Flanagan, and Vanderwood (1997) that the Gf-Gc theory advocated by Carroll is the "most useful framework for understanding cognitive functioning" (p. 194).

Relationships Between CAS and the Wechsler Scales

Naglieri and Das (1997c) provide information about the relationships between the CAS and two Wechsler Scales (WISC-III and WPPSI-R). There were four studies conducted during the final stages of the test's develop-

Table 5.6 Relationships Between Wechsler Scales and Cognitive Assessment System

Scale	Group	N	CAS	FSIQ	Correlation
WISC-III	Regular Ed	54	106	105	.69
WISC-III	LD	81	88	90	.71
WISC-III	MR	84	66	61	.66
WPPSI-R	Regular Ed	33	98	90	.60
Medians	All Samples	252	93	90	.68

Note. LD = learning disabled; MR = mentally retarded. All correlations are significant at $p < .01$. Data are from Naglieri and Das (1997c).

ment, the results of which are summarized in Table 5.6. These results show that the CAS FS and WISC-III FSIQ mean scores were similar for groups of children in regular education classes as well as those identified as learning disabled (LD) and mentally retarded (MR). The CAS FS and WPPSI-R FSIQ mean scores were also similar for a sample of children in regular education settings. The correlations between the two tests' total scores shown in Table 5.6 ranged from .60 to .71 (median = .68). This indicates that the CAS is significantly correlated with the WISC-III and WPPSI-R, but that the relationship is not as highly related as is typically found when traditional IQ tests are correlated.

Profiles for Exceptional Children

When examining the relationships between scores on the CAS and traditional tests, the issue of profiles for exceptional children should be considered. This is easily accomplished by consulting the various test manuals. Summary results are presented in Chapter 6 of this text. The results strongly suggest that the CAS yields profiles that separate, for example, children with Attention-Deficit Hyperactivity Disorder (ADHD) from those with reading disabilities. This is not the case for the Wechsler or Woodcock-Johnson tests.

Treatment Validity

School psychologists have become increasingly interested in the relevance of ability test results to instruction as well as specific interventions (Braden,

1997). The topic, which was ignored by Carroll in his review of PASS, is important and is addressed here. The value of linking assessment to intervention was noted by Braden (1997) when he stated that the concept of "treatment validity will be the next standard incorporated into test manuals [as it has been done in the] Cognitive Assessment System" (p. 243). In the *Cognitive Assessment System Interpretive Handbook*, and in this book, the matching of interventions to test scores (referred to as treatment validity) has been illustrated and supported by published research. Contrary to statements by Esters, Ittenbach, and Han (1997) that "attempts to establish the treatment validity of . . . the CAS, have met with little success" (p. 217), there is good evidence that PASS is related to instruction.

The concept behind evaluation of the treatment validity of PASS is the determination of whether children learn best when given an intervention that addresses their cognitive need. Does information about a child's PASS profile have relevance to the type of instruction given; and if the child's characteristics are taken into consideration, can the teacher maximize learning? One of the purposes of special education should be to provide specialized instruction that works best for the child. If CAS results provide the teacher with instructionally relevant information about the child, then the instrument has some treatment validity. There have been two published studies and one recently completed study that illustrate the relevance of PASS to instruction. These results are summarized here, but for more information on the methods used, see Chapter 7 of this text.

Naglieri and Gottling (1995, 1997) published two investigations that showed the relevance of PASS to math instruction. Both studies were designed to determine if children who are poor in math calculation and planning would benefit from an instruction to teach them to be more planful. The logic is as follows: If children who are poor in planning are taught to be more planful when doing an academic task that requires a lot of planning (e.g., math calculation), then they should improve in the academic task. If children are not poor in planning, then the instruction designed to teach them to be more planful will not have as much influence because the instruction does not match their cognitive need. Moreover, if the purpose of the instruction is to teach children to be more planful, this instruction should not be especially helpful to children who are low in the other processes. In that case there would be a mismatch between the child and the instruction. For example, one would not expect much improvement in a child with a low score in Simultaneous processing who is given a planning-based instruction because he or she does not necessarily need this type of instruction.

Both of Naglieri and Gottling's studies demonstrated that children who earned low scores on the CAS Planning subtests improved considerably in math calculation taken directly from the classroom curriculum when provided an instruction that encouraged their use of strategies or plans. In contrast, children who were good in Planning showed modest improvement (about half as much) when provided exactly the same instruction. No similar relationships were found between Attention, Simultaneous, Successive, or Wechsler IQ scores. These results are consistent with earlier research by Cormier, Carlson, and Das (1990) and Kar, Dash, Das, and Carlson (1992). Those studies found that children who were poor in Planning benefited from an instruction that was designed to help them be more planful, but that children who were not poor in Planning did not show such improvement. These studies illustrate that there is evidence for a connection between PASS and instruction.

Does the PASS Theory Have Factor Analytic Support?

Since the publication of Carroll's review in 1995, the question of factorial support for the PASS theory has been amply addressed using the test's standardization sample ($N = 2,200$). Because the data are presented in the *CAS Interpretive Handbook* (Naglieri & Das, 1997c), only some of the results are summarized here. Naglieri and Das (1997c) provide strong evidence from confirmatory factor analytic investigations that a four-factor PASS configuration of the 12 subtests provided the best fit to the data. The one-, two-, and three-factor solutions were not adequate, and the four-factor model was a significant improvement over the competing three-factor solutions. The four-factor PASS model exceeded all standards for model fit (e.g., AGFIs above .80 and RMS less than .10). Thus it appears that because Carroll's conclusions were based on (a) his re-analysis of old experimental test data in early published results, (b) experimental tests not included in the final version of the CAS, and (c) experimental tests that have been changed considerably, his conclusions do not apply to the way in which PASS constructs are operationalized in the CAS.

The question of factorial support for the PASS theory also must be put into perspective. How important is factorial support, and do other sources of evidence matter? Some researchers have argued that factorial support is not a sufficient criterion for establishing the validity of a theory and that this method has limitation. For example, McGrew, Keith, Flanagan, and Vanderwood (1997) remind readers that

> some of the major limitations of Gf-Gc theory are that (a) the theory is largely a descriptive empirical generalization of research findings and much less a deductive explanation of thee findings, (b) the structure implied for the Gf-Gc factors in rotation factor solutions is most likely *not* [emphasis added] a good indication of the organization of actual human abilities, (c) the theory is largely a product of linear equations (viz., factor analysis), while natural phenomena most likely are nonlinear in nature, and (d) the theory provides little information on how the Gf-Gc abilities develop or how the cognitive processes work together. (p. 194)

Thus factor analytic support is not a litmus test for a theory of ability, nor a test like the CAS. This is not to say it is unimportant, but it must be considered with other relevant forms of validity—for example, prediction to achievement, differential profiles for different children, and treatment validity.

It is reasonable to conclude that the validity of the PASS theory, or any theory, must be examined from several perspectives. What role does factor analysis play in this case? Probably the most value it has in this context is in evaluating the correspondence of the subtests to the scales a test yields. Factor analysis provides information about how subtests group together (or factor), which can support or fail to support the organization of subtests into scales. This helps determine if there is empirical support (based on correlation) for combining several subtests into one scale. If adequate support for the structure of the test is found, practitioners can have confidence that the subtests included in a particular scale (Planning, for example) do have something in common and can be combined into a composite score.

The purpose of the factor analytic investigations reported in the *Cognitive Assessment System Interpretive Handbook* was to examine the correspondence of the subtests in the test to the organization of the scale based on the PASS theory. It is important to note that the PASS theory guided the production and selection of subtests during development of the CAS. In the early work on PASS (see Das, Kirby, & Jarman, 1979; Das, Naglieri, & Kirby, 1994), factor analysis was not used to discover what to measure or include in the test; this was outlined by Luria's description of the three functional units. Factor analysis was used to examine the efficiency of the experimental tests as measures of each of the PASS processes.

The reason the CAS subtests were examined using factor analysis was to test the correspondence between the subtests and the scales on which they were assigned. To accomplish this goal a series of confirmatory factor analyses was conducted. The correspondence of the standardization data to the anticipated organization of subtests was assessed through a group of methods called fit statistics. These results showed that there was "a good fit between the PASS model and the data from each of four age groups" (Naglieri & Das, 1997c, p. 53). In addition, there is good evidence and theoretical rationale that the four-factor PASS model is the most appropriate way to interpret the 12 CAS subtests. For more details on factorial studies of the CAS, see Naglieri and Das (1997c, Chapter 4) and Naglieri (in press).

CONCLUSIONS

This chapter attempts to provide a balanced review of the strengths and weaknesses of the CAS. The text discusses published reviews of the PASS theory and the test as well as recent comments by researchers in school psychology. These reviews generally suggest that the CAS offers important advantages to the practitioner. This is especially seen in the different profiles for ADHD and reading disabled children as well as the implications for intervention. No other test of this type has been shown to have these advantages. From the perspective of Carroll (1995) the PASS theory was not well supported, but evidence he did not consider in his review and evidence obtained since his review contradict his arguments. Moreover, because his review was essentially based on factor analysis, and there are several other sources of evidence in support of PASS theory and the CAS, his concerns have less weight when viewed in perspective. More importantly, when PASS theory and the CAS are examined from a broader perspective, as done by Anastasi and Urbina (1997), Gindis (1996), and Roodin (1996), a positive outlook is suggested. This is why Gindis viewed the work "as a landmark event in the field of educational/school psychology" (p. 305).

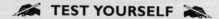 **TEST YOURSELF**

1. **The validity of a theory and test can be established by one method such as factor analysis.** True or False

2. **There is good evidence that CAS Planning subtests are not measures of speed, as suggested by Carroll (1995).** True or False

3. **The CAS Full Scale correlates higher with achievement than do tests such as the WISC-III and WJ-R Cognitive.** True or False

4. **ADHD and LD children have different PASS Scale profiles.** True or False

5. **The CAS has important implications for intervention.** True or False

Answers: 1. False; 2. True; 3. True; 4. True; 5. True

Six

CLINICAL APPLICATIONS OF THE CAS*

CHILDREN WITH LEARNING DISABILITIES

Children with learning disabilities constitute the largest group that receives special educational services, and therefore it is very important to accurately identify these individuals. This population is included in the category Specific Learning Disability in the most recent federal regulations. According to the Individuals with Disabilities Education Act (IDEA; Public Law 105-17) of 1997, the term *Specific Learning Disability* (SLD) means:

> A disorder in one or more of the *basic psychological processes* [emphasis added] involved in understanding or in using language, spoken or written, which disorder may manifest itself in imperfect ability to listen, speak, read, write, spell, or do mathematical calculations. Such term includes such conditions as perceptual disabilities, brain injury, minimal brain dysfunction, dyslexia, and developmental aphasia. Such term does not include a learning problem that is primarily the result of visual, hearing, or motor disabilities, or mental retardation, of emotional disturbance, or of environmental, cultural, or economic disadvantage. (p. 46)

The conceptualization of SLD presented in IDEA is also consistent with the definition proposed earlier by the National Joint Committee for Learning Disabilities (NJCLD; Hammill, Leigh, McNutt, & Larsen, 1981):

> Learning Disabilities is a generic term that refers to a heterogeneous group of disorders manifested by significant difficulties in the acquisition and use of listening, speaking, reading, writing, reasoning or mathematical abilities. These disorders are intrinsic to the individual and pre-

*This chapter coauthored by Jack A. Naglieri and James C. Kaufman.

≡ Rapid Reference

Traditional IQ

- yields a discrepancy which tells that the IQ and achievement are not consistent.
- involves defining the LD child on the basis of *not* finding any intellectual reason for the academic failure.

CAS and PASS

- yield a discrepancy which tells that a child's achievement and PASS processes are discrepant.
- yield a cognitive weakness which tells that a child's achievement and some specific PASS processes are consistent.
- identify a consistency which tells if there is a cognitive explanation for the academic problem.

sumed to be due to central nervous system dysfunction. Even though a learning disability may occur concomitantly with other handicapping conditions (e.g., sensory impairment, mental retardation, social and emotional disturbance) or environmental influences (e.g., cultural differences, insufficient/inappropriate instruction, psychogenic factors), it is not the direct result of those conditions or influences. (p. 336)

The identification of a difficulty with basic psychological processes is not easily obtained with tests such as the Wechsler because it is built on the general ability model, and the subtests were included because they were non-specific. This leads to difficulties in finding distinctive profiles at the subtest level for children with specific disabilities (Kavale & Forness, 1984; Mueller, Dennis, & Short, 1986). Swanson (1991) argues that this may be the most serious limitation of IQ tests because "these measures obscure the specific discrepancies we are trying to find" (p. 3). Given that traditional IQ tests were constructed to measure ability from a general intelligence perspective and not to examine specific psychological processes, it should not be surprising that it is difficult to use them for that purpose. In contrast, the CAS was designed to measure specific psychological processes as defined by the PASS theory and therefore is amply suited for identification of SLD children on this basis. Thus a child's low processing score (e.g., the cognitive weakness) can be used to determine if a child has a "disorder in one or more of the basic psychological processes" (p. 46, IDEA) or a dysfunction in basic cognitive processing (as described by NJCLD) related to the academic failure.

Children with learning disabilities have typically been identified on the basis of a discrepancy between ability (IQ scores) and achievement, and a psychological processing disorder (Reynolds, 1990). When a discrepancy is found between IQ and achievement, this means that the ability measure did not predict the (low) level of achievement for an individual child. In other words, the IQ test was not sensitive to an intellectual problem that might be responsible for the academic failure; otherwise there would have been a discrepancy and a consistency. The CAS allows for identification of both a discrepancy (low achievement with high processing) and a consistency (a cognitive weakness that is consistent with the level of achievement), as illustrated in Chapter 4. When a referred child has a significant PASS profile (e.g., a cognitive weakness) along with a discrepancy between the high PASS score and achievement, and a consistency between the PASS cognitive weakness and achievement, then support for the SLD diagnosis is obtained. (See Rapid Reference on page 134.) It is important to note, however, that the CAS results would not only help determine eligibility (diagnosis) and establish the relationship between academic failure and a psychological process disorder, but also help to guide interventions (see Chapter 7).

Naglieri and Das (1997c) present research on the identification of children with SLD. They describe a study of children with SLD in the *Cognitive Assessment System Interpretive Handbook*. They found that children with SLD in reading decoding earned low scores on the Successive processing scale, as anticipated. These results, along with data for children with Attention-Deficit Hyperactivity Disorder, are presented in the following section. The CAS profiles of these children are also presented because of the challenges posed by separation of these groups and the similarity of their profiles on traditional IQ tests.

CHILDREN WITH ATTENTION-DEFICIT HYPERACTIVITY DISORDER

The accurate diagnosis of children with learning disabilities and attention deficits through the use of IQ tests has been of interest to researchers and practitioners for some time. Traditional IQ tests have been used to try to identify these children, but there is controversy about the effectiveness of these tools for diagnostic purposes. Most research on the differentiation of groups based on IQ Scale profiles has found little support (Kavale & Forness, 1984; Mueller, Dennis, & Short, 1986). Because the CAS provides a broader approach to examination of a child's cognitive profile that is theory driven, the opportunity for obtaining more distinctive profiles is possible. There is some indication that the CAS may yield different profiles for different types of exceptional children. But before this research can be examined, it is important to consider the definitions of ADHD that have been offered and relate them to the PASS theory.

The *Diagnostic and Statistical Manual of Mental Disorders* (4th ed., American Psychiatric Association, 1994) describes Attention-Deficit Hyperactivity Disorder as having three types: Predominantly Hyperactive-Impulsive, Predominantly Inattentive, and Combined types. These three disorders include Inattentive problems such as failing to (a) maintain and sustain attention, (b) follow directions, and (c) avoid distractions. Hyperactive-Impulsive difficulties involve (a) fidgeting, (b) excessive restlessness and talking, and (c) inability to take turns and regulate behavior. The criteria for these three types of Attention Deficit are listed in Rapid Reference on page 137.

Barkley (1994) describes ADHD as a "delay in the development of response inhibition . . . [and an] inefficiency in the neuropsychological functions that we believe inhibit responding" (p. vii). He further describes the disorder as a "profound disturbance in self-regulation and organization of behavior across time" (p. vii), often described as executive functions and associated

CAUTION

Identification of children with ADHD through the use of the Wechsler Scale Index or subtests is not recommended by researchers who study Attention-Deficit Disorder because the test is not sensitive to the problems these children have.

⩵ *Rapid Reference*

Diagnostic Criteria for Attention-Deficit Disorders

Inattentive

(a) often fails to give close attention to details or makes careless mistakes in schoolwork, work, or other activities

(b) often has difficulty sustaining attention in tasks or play activities

(c) often does not seem to listen when spoken to directly

(d) often does not follow through on instructions and fails to finish school-work, chores, or duties in the workplace (not due to oppositional behavior or failure to understand instructions)

(e) often has difficulty organizing tasks and activities

(f) often avoids, dislikes, or is reluctant to engage in tasks that require sustained mental effort (e.g., schoolwork or homework)

(g) often loses things necessary for tasks or activities (e.g., toys, school assignments, pencils, books, or tools)

(h) is often easily distracted by extraneous stimuli

(i) is often forgetful in daily activities

Hyperactive-Impulsive

(a) often fidgets with hands or feet or squirms in seat

(b) often leaves seat in classroom or in other situations in which remaining seated is expected

(c) often runs about or climbs excessively in situations in which it is inappropriate (in adolescents or adults, may be limited to subjective feelings of restlessness)

(d) often has difficulty playing or engaging in leisure activities quietly

(e) is often "on the go" or often acts as if "driven by a motor"

(f) often talks excessively

(g) often blurts out answers before questions have been completed

(h) often has difficulty awaiting turn

(i) often interrupts or intrudes on others (e.g., butts into conversations or games)

Note. From American Psychiatric Association (1994).

with the prefrontal regions of the brain. This view is consistent with other researchers' findings that ADHD is related to impaired functioning of the frontal lobes (e.g., Hynd, Voeller, Hern, & Marshall, 1991).

In light of the PASS theory, the description of ADHD summarized above suggests that these children have difficulty with Planning (self-

DON'T FORGET

When talking about Attention-Deficit Disorder, it is logical to assume that the problem is with attention; but researchers have found that children with ADHD cannot control their behavior and have inattention problems that are related to Planning and Attention as described in PASS.

regulation, inhibition of responses, control of behavior) as measured in the CAS. Attention subtest scores are also expected to be low for these children, but especially for those with the Inattentive type of ADHD because of their difficulty with sustaining attention and resisting distraction. In contrast, the general ability approach taken by traditional IQ tests does not seem to lend itself to identification of these particular issues. This is apparent when the literature on identification of ADHD is examined.

Identification of children with ADHD through the use of traditional IQ tests has been studied for many years by many researchers. Barkley's (1994) summary of research on the Wechlser scales led him to conclude that because ADHD is characterized by "behavioral disinhibition and poor self regulation" (p. 171), which are not measured by the test, including the Freedom From Distractibility (FFD) factor, that test is not recommended "in assessing attention or in establishing evidence for or against a diagnosis of ADHD" (p. 331). Moreover, DuPaul and Stoner (1994) conclude that the Wechsler scales have "not been found to reliably discriminate ADHD from normal children or students with Learning Disabilities" (p. 24). These authors, and others, have found that identification of ADHD through use of the Wechsler is problematic because the test does not measure those cognitive aspects of a child that are associated with ADHD. To gain additional perspective, it is useful to examine information drawn from the WISC-IIII (Wechsler, 1991) and CAS (Naglieri & Das, 1997c) test manuals and a recent publication by Woodcock (1998). See also Rapid Reference on page 139.

In the WISC-III manual, Wechsler (1991) describes three studies involving children with unspecified Learning Disabilities ($n = 65$), children with spe-

☰ Rapid Reference

Executive Functions That Are Disrupted by ADHD

1. inhibition of inappropriate responding
2. sustaining information in working memory
3. anticipating consequence of actions
4. establishing goals and plans of action
5. avoiding reacting to stimuli that interfere with goal-directed behavior
6. demonstrating self-regulated and goal-directed behavior
7. regulating affect and motivation

Note. From DuPaul and Stoner (1994).

cific Reading Disabilities ($n = 34$), and children with Attention-Deficit Hyperactivity Disorder ($n = 68$). The ADHD group was identified using DSM-III-R (American Psychiatric Association, 1987) criteria. The mean WISC-III Index scores earned by these groups are shown in Figure 6.1. The results show that the profiles for the LD, RD, and ADHD children were essentially the same. The RD and ADHD group means differed only slightly, and the LD and ADHD differed in elevation but not in shape of the profile. These results suggest that the Wechsler Scale profiles for these children from different groups do not differ, as was suggested by Barkley (1990). A similar result is found for the WJ-R Tests of Cognitive Ability.

Woodcock (1998) provides information about the scores earned by children with Learning Disabilities ($n = 62$) and Attention-Deficit Disorders ($n = 67$) for the seven Gf-Gc clusters based on the WJ-R cognitive tests. The means for the seven clusters, provided in Figure 6.2, show that like the WISC-III, the LD and ADHD samples have similar score profiles. The scores across the seven clusters show little differentiation between the samples.

Naglieri and Das (1997c) provide two studies of children with ADHD ($n = 66$) and Specific Learning Disabilities ($n = 24$). The ADHD children were all identified according to DSM-IV criteria and a battery of tests. The sample of children with Attention-Deficit Hyperactivity Disorder was carefully selected following DSM-IV criteria. Children with other comorbid diagnosis such as conduct disorders, anxiety disorders, or oppositional defiant disorders were

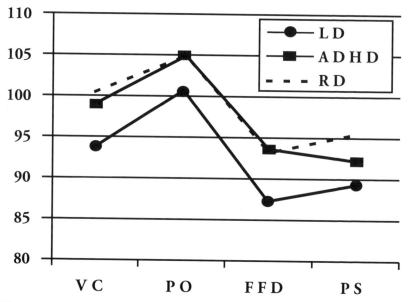

Figure 6.1   Comparison of WISC-III Index Scores for Children with Learning Disabilities, Attention-Deficit Hyperactivity Disorder, and Reading Disabilities

Note. VC = Verbal Comprehension; PO = Perceptual Organization; FFD = Freedom from Distractibility; PS = Processing Speed. Data are from Wechsler (1991).

excluded from the study. The sample of children with reading disabilities was selected on the basis of a discrepancy between the WISC-III Full Scale IQ and the WJ-R Word Attack subtest of 15 points and a Word Attack score of less than 90. The mean PASS scores these children earned on the CAS, provided in Figure 6.3, show a different pattern for these two groups. Additionally, these results are different than those obtained for the Wechsler and Woodcock tests.

The results of the studies provided by the respective test authors suggest that the PASS theory and CAS provide a useful and unique perspective from which to view and assess ADHD and SLD. The differences found on the CAS between SLD and ADHD are in contrast findings of previous research with traditional IQ tests. This is not unexpected if the nature of ADHD is considered from the perspective of the PASS theory. That is, if ADHD is a failure of inhibition of responses and self-control, which are associated with the frontal region of the brain, then low scores on Planning, with depressed Attention

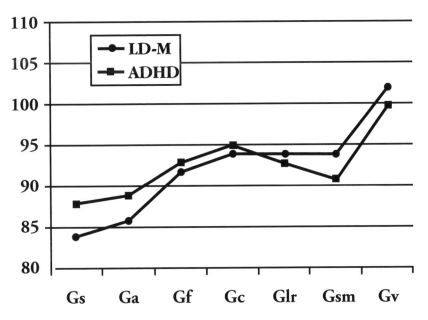

Figure 6.2 Comparison of WJ-R Cognitive Scores for Children with Learning Disabilities and Attention-Deficit Hyperactivity Disorder

Note. Gs = Processing Speed; Ga = Auditory Processing; Gf = Fluid Reasoning; Gc = Comprehension Knowledge; Glr = Long-term Retrieval; Gsm = Short-term Memory; and Gv = Visual Processing. Data are from Woodcock (1998).

DON'T FORGET

The focus of CAS interpretation is on the PASS profiles rather than CAS subtest score variability because the test is based on theory; interpretation of scores yielded by the test should also be based on theory. Examination of CAS profiles, therefore, focuses on the PASS scales rather than on the subtest profiles.

scores, are logical and consistent with current understanding of the disorder. Although the ADHD Inattentive type has not been studied in the same way, individual cases have shown markedly depressed scores in the CAS Attention scale for individuals described as fitting in this category (see Rapid Reference on page 143).

The results for children with SLD are different from those obtained for individuals with ADHD. The reading disabled group had

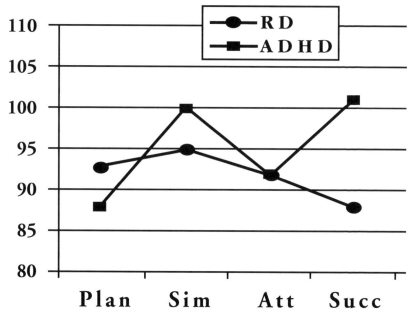

Figure 6.3 Comparison of CAS PASS Scores for Children with Reading Disabilities and Attention-Deficit Hyperactivity Disorder

Note. Plan = Planning; Sim = Simultaneous; Att = Attention; Succ = Successive. Data are from Naglieri and Das (1997c).

poor performance on the Successive Scale. These results are consistent with the view that children with reading decoding failure and phonological coding problems perform poorly in Successive processing (Das, Naglieri, & Kirby, 1994). These authors suggest that Successive processing problems and poor reading decoding are associated because assembly of correct sounds in order (e.g., sounding out words) demands Successive processing.

The examination of SLD and ADHD studies suggests that the PASS theory as represented by the CAS offers a different perspective on the relative strengths and needs of these children. Moreover, the profiles that have been obtained are consistent with previous research and views of the nature of the learning problems these individuals experience.

INDIVIDUALS WITH MENTAL RETARDATION

There has been a longstanding dissatisfaction with the concept of intelligence and its measurement among those who work with individuals with mental re-

Rapid Reference

....

Illustration of Selected Test Scores for a Child with Inattention Problems

Male age 12 years 6 months

WISC-III

VIQ = 117

PIQ = 121

FSIQ = 121

WRAT

Reading = 82

Spelling = 84

Math = 108

CAS

Planning = 104

Simultaneous = 110

Attention = 63

Successive = 86

tardation (Das & Naglieri, 1996). Some researchers have even attempted to redefine mental retardation without using an IQ criterion (e.g., Green, Mackay, McIlvane, Saunders, & Sraci, 1990), but these alternatives have not been widely accepted. Despite the concerns, practitioners have continued to rely on traditional measures of IQ to evaluate intelligence for persons suspected of having mental retardation. Notwithstanding their limitations, these tests offer reliable methods, adequate predictive validity, and excellent standardization samples.

There are two advantages of the CAS in evaluating a person for mental retardation. First, it provides assessment that requires minimal acquired knowledge. This ensures that the individual cannot fail the test for lack of facts typically obtained from school (e.g., vocabulary, arithmetic, and general information). Second, the CAS measures a broad range of cognitive processes, which can assist in differential diagnosis. Especially important are Planning and Attention because, as suggested by Das, Naglieri, and Kirby (1994), planning is related to some aspects of adaptive functioning, and adaptive behavior scores have not been consistent with traditional IQ tests. This is illustrated in cases where children earn low IQ scores and experience academic failure but *do* function adequately outside of school. From the PASS perspective, this means that children with low achievement and possibly low Simultaneous processing (such as PIQ) but adequate Planning and Attention can do poorly academically but well outside of school.

Only one study has examined the performance of individuals with mental retardation on the CAS (Naglieri & Das, 1997c). In this investigation 84

Table 6.1 CAS and WISC-III Scores Obtained for Children With Mental Retardation

		Mean	Standard deviation
WISC-III			
	VQ	62.6	10.1
	PIQ	65.0	9.5
	FSIQ	60.7	9.1
CAS			
	Planning	74.0	11.9
	Simultaneous	70.9	9.9
	Attention	77.3	12.3
	Successive	72.8	16.5
	FS	65.9	11.4

Note. Data are from Naglieri and Das (1997c).

children with mental retardation were administered the CAS and WISC-III. All standard scores were very low, as expected for this population, and both tests yielded low Full Scale scores. The WISC-III Full Scale score was 61 and the CAS Full Scale score was 66 (see Table 6.1). These results suggest that the use of subtests that do not rely on verbal achievement likely led to the lower WISC-III standard scores.

These initial results suggest that the CAS is a viable tool for assessment of individuals who may have mental retardation. The Full Scale score is likely to be similar to that obtained from the Wechsler, and perhaps slightly higher, especially for persons with low scores in verbal/achievement subtests. This separation of achievement from ability is a very important distinction for this population (Das & Naglieri, 1996), and one that can lead to more accurate identification of individuals with mental retardation.

INDIVIDUALS WITH TRAUMATIC BRAIN INJURY

Children who experience traumatic brain injury (TBI) typically have cognitive deficits that include impairments in concentration, attention, memory, executive functions, and academic and social functioning (Savage & Wolcott, 1994). Especially influenced are what are often described as executive functions (Begali, 1992; Sattler, 1988) or planning (Naglieri & Das, 1997c). Typically intelligence tests such as the Wechsler scales are used to evaluate these children. However, researchers have cautioned that "head injured children often show significant processing and learning disorders despite normal Full Scale IQ values, comparable Verbal and Performance Scale results, and no significant subtest scatter" (Baxter, Cohen, & Ylvisaker, 1985, p. 255). Others have argued that traditional methods may not be able to detect the specific effects of TBI (Telzrow, 1991) and that IQ scores may overestimate the child's functioning and show little sensitivity to specific deficits (Lehr, 1990). These positions are logical if it is assumed that traditional IQ tests do not measure planning and attention, which are considered the primary problems for children with TBI (Savage & Wolcott, 1994).

The utility of the CAS for identification of children with TBI was recently studied by Gutentag, Naglieri, and Yeates (1998). Their sample of 44 children included 22 who had sustained a TBI and a control group ($n = 22$). The children in the TBI group all experienced closed head injuries of moderate to severe magnitude, as defined by the number of days of impaired consciousness following their injuries. Each TBI child was matched to a control subject selected from the CAS standardization sample on the basis of age, gender, race, and geographic region.

The results of the study showed that the deficits that children with TBI displayed in Planning and Attention were detected with the CAS. The results are consistent with expectations that children with TBI would have significant deficits in Planning and Attention when compared to a matched group of controls. These children earned significantly lower scores in Planning and Attention (see Figure 6.4). The results suggest that even though children with TBI sometimes function adequately on tests of general intelligence, persistent deficits in Attention and Planning were found. The results are consistent with the underlying neuropathology associated with TBI in children (Hynd, Voeller, Hern, & Marshall, 1991).

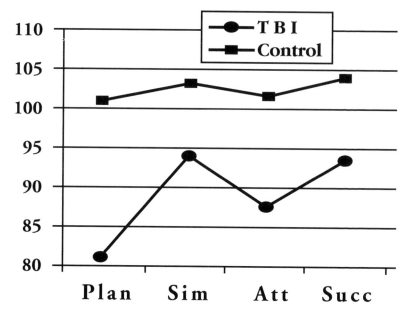

Figure 6.4 Comparison of CAS PASS Scores for Children with Traumatic Brain Injury and the Control sample

Note. Plan = Planning; Sim = Simultaneous; Att = Attention; Succ = Successive. Data are from Gutentag, Naglieri, and Yeates (1998).

GIFTED CHILDREN

Definitions of intellectual giftedness have varied nearly as much as the definitions of intelligence itself. Giftedness has been defined as occurring in a strict percentage of individuals on the basis of measured intelligence. Some broader interpretations include such constructs as creativity and motivation, whereas other definitions are mere terminologies developed for practical social policy use (Robinson & Clinkenbeard, 1998). The need to measure and identify exceptional ability goes back as far as the need to measure intelligence. Whereas Alfred Binet developed his tests to single out intellectually inferior students, Francis Galton's mental tests were designed to identify superior individuals and demonstrate the genetics of greatness. (See Rapid Reference on page 147.)

It is often harder to assess gifted students accurately on standard instruments for several reasons. For example, there is considerable variability in their

Giftedness as Defined by Public Law 95-561

- Intellectual Ability
- Creative Thinking
- Leadership Ability
- Visual and Performing Arts Ability
- Specific Ability Aptitude

intelligence test scores. This was shown by Wilkinson (1993), who examined a large sample of third-grade students with IQs higher than 120 on the Wechsler Intelligence Scale for Children—Revised (WISC-R) and found that their test profiles were more varied than the norm. The gifted students had larger verbal-performance discrepancies and evidenced more scatter in their subtest scores.

Another problem in identification relates to the nature of the gifted child. Many cognitive theorists argue that the essential element in understanding gifted children involves looking at the higher-level processes (Sternberg & Davidson, 1986). One such higher-level cognitive process often used to distinguish gifted from non-gifted children is planning ability. Schofield and Ashman (1987) tested 323 fifth and sixth grade students and found that gifted students were significantly better at tasks of high-level planning than a group of above-average students. Similarly, Grover (1987) studied computer competency in gifted and non-gifted students and found that the best predictor of ability to solve complex problems was planning skills. Thus these authors have found planning to be an important part of giftedness, but traditional intelligence tests do not measure planning (Das, Naglieri, & Kirby, 1994). This was also suggested by McCallum and Karnes (1987), who tested gifted students on the WISC-R or Stanford-Binet and a measure of planning. They found little overlap between scores on the intelligence tests and scores on the measure of planning.

One link between giftedness and planning can be found in metacognition, the act of thinking about one's cognitive processes (Flavell, 1979). Metacognition has long been recognized as a key component of giftedness. Borkowski and Peck (1986) have studied the importance of metamemory and giftedness. Alexander, Carr, and Schwanenflugel (1995) found evidence that gifted students possess more factual knowledge of metacognition than do non-gifted students. However, there was little difference between gifted and non-gifted students in cognitive monitoring.

Metacognition is also a central aspect of planning. For example, a student who scores high in Planning is aware of the task-strategy relationship and monitors strategic success—two essential aspects of metacognition (Das, Naglieri, & Kirby, 1994). Metacognition is often cited as one of the most researchable aspects of giftedness. Yet any intelligence test that overlooks planning also fails to recognize this pivotal way of distinguishing gifted from nongifted students.

Further evidence of the link between giftedness and planning is revealed through research on creativity. Albert and Runco (1986) argue that at high levels of ability and talent it is often difficult to separate intelligence from creativity. Certainly the strong link between the two constructs is well established (Barron & Harrington, 1981). The relationship between the two, though substantial, is non-linear. That is to say, empirical evidence suggests that intelligence is an essential, but not sufficient, component of creative ability up to a point—often shown to be about an IQ of 120; however, IQs above 120 do not lead to greater creativity (Getzels & Jackson, 1962).

The important role of planning in creativity is found in both empirical studies and in philosophical theory. Redmund, Mumford, and Teach (1993) found that more time spent planning and re-planning a project led to more productivity and higher creativity. Guastello, Shissler, Driscoll, and Hyde (1998) studied eight cognitive styles and found that the planner style was significantly positively correlated with creative productivity.

Researchers who have studied creative cognition, such as Finke, Ward, and Smith (1992) and Amabile (1983, 1996), recognize the importance of planning. Finke and his colleagues propose two central cognitive processes that contribute to creativity. One is generation of the idea, and the other is evaluation of the idea. Both processes require significant planning for successful execution. Similarly, Amabile's componential theory of creativity shows the influence of planning. Her three components are domain-relevant skills (i.e., knowledge, technical skills), task motivation, and creativity-relevant skills. It is in the latter component that the importance of planning can be seen. Creativity-relevant skills include exploring new pathways, keeping response options open for as long as possible, and suspending judgment. These skills reflect not only an individual's potential creativity but also his or her ability to plan.

CONCLUSIONS

The CAS is useful in evaluating clinical cases even though much additional research is needed. The data provided here offer important insights into how various children perform on the PASS tasks. Moreover, they suggest that the CAS and PASS theory could be used to identify particular types of exceptional children and redefine the nature of some of these special individuals.

✒ TEST YOURSELF ✒

1. **Children with reading disabilities have a weakness in which of the PASS processes?**
   (a) Planning
   (b) Simultaneous
   (c) Attention
   (d) Successive

2. **Children with Attention-Deficit Disorders Hyperactive-Impulsive and Combined types have poor scores in**
   (a) Planning and Successive.
   (b) Simultaneous and Successive.
   (c) Attention.
   (d) Planning and Attention.

3. **Children with Attention-Deficit Disorders Inattentive type have poor scores in**
   (a) Planning and Successive.
   (b) Simultaneous and Successive.
   (c) Attention.
   (d) Planning and Attention.

4. **Children with Attention-Deficit Disorder Hyperactive-Impulsive type have difficulty with**
   (a) self-control.
   (b) paying attention.
   (c) resisting distractions.
   (d) spatial tasks.

5. Creativity in gifted children seems to be related to which PASS process?

(a) Planning

(b) Simultaneous

(c) Attention

(d) Successive

Answers: 1. d; 2. d; 3. c; 4. a; 5. a

Seven

MAKING THE CONNECTION BETWEEN PASS AND INTERVENTION*

THE TEACHING-LEARNING ENVIRONMENT

Every situation in which learning and problem solving occur involves a learner, a teacher, a setting, and information to be learned. For a preschool child, a mother or other caregiver might be the teacher, the home might be the setting, and knowledge about what the mother does when the child cries might be the curriculum. At school, there is a student, a teacher, the classroom, and the content of various disciplines to be mastered. On the job, the employee might be the learner, the teacher might be an expert or a supervisor or a co-worker, the workplace is the setting, and specialized knowledge required for the job is the curriculum. In some situations, the teacher might not be a person but a book or technical manual.

These four agents act interdependently to facilitate or inhibit learning. At one time all agents may be in equilibrium, and at other times there may be an imbalance, or a deficit, that reduces the effectiveness of the teaching-learning process. For example, the student may have a fever, the teacher may not have prepared the lesson, there may be noisy construction taking place outside the classroom, or there may be insufficient or inappropriate material available to help students master the content. Some of the factors that affect learning are listed in Table 7.1.

Teaching and learning constitute an ecosystem in which there is a series of inputs, teaching and learning events, and a series of outputs. The concept of ecology is important because it focuses on the interdependence of all influences, rather than isolating one agent as a potential problem source. In other words, if a student cannot learn it is not necessarily the student's fault. It

---

*This chapter was coauthored by Jack A. Naglieri and Adrian F. Ashman.

Table 7.1 Agents and Their Characteristics That Influence Learning Outcomes

The Learner

Heredity (one's genetic endowment)

Health or physical condition

Prior learning (content, strategies)

Cognitive processes (e.g., PASS dimensions)

Personality

Comfort within the learning setting

Motivation and self-perception

Family's expressed views about education

Disposition toward teacher and peers

Receptivity toward content and learning

Cultural or ethnic background

Attributions of success and failure

Social and interpersonal skills

Responsiveness to disruption

Behavior patterns

Gender

The Teacher

Teaching experience

Self-confidence and disposition to teaching

Familiarity with content

Emotional and physical well-being

Ability to communicate with and stimulate students

Conflict resolution/behavior management skills

Interest in meeting students' needs

Administrative pressures

Knowledge of students' needs

Personal support network

The Setting

Size and set-up of the classroom

Equipment and teaching resources

Weather, temperature, and light

Quality of interactions between learners and teachers

Interruptions and disruptions

Number of students and teachers present

Time of day

Emotional climate within the setting

Characteristics of the student body

Cultural context

The Curriculum

Complexity of content (e.g., abstract, concrete)

Amount of information to be learned per time unit

Table 7.1 continued

Structure of the knowledge base (e.g., hierarchical, relational)	Assessment requirements
	Strategies needed and provided
Dependence on previously acquired knowledge	Relevant curriculum resources
Outcome requirements (e.g., repetition, understanding, application)	

might be because the teacher is unable to adequately address a student's learning disability, the curriculum materials are not stimulating or engaging, or the student is sitting beside a friend who constantly interrupts.

It is important to remember, however, that knowing about the PASS cognitive competencies or deficiencies of a learner is a critical element in a complex process that leads to effective teaching and learning. With the redefinition of ability based on the CAS, there is still a need for a holistic view of the student's processing characteristics and personal circumstances, as well as the teaching-learning environment in which the student is expected to perform. Therefore it is recommended that the psychologist, in collaboration with the classroom teacher and other appropriate individuals, evaluate the wide range of contextual characteristics listed in Table 7.1.

IMPROVING LEARNING: WHAT THE CAS CAN TELL

The CAS provides a window into the way in which people think, learn, and solve problems. Each learner develops and uses these processes in accordance with his or her biological makeup and learning experiences within a social-cultural context. On the basis of considerable data (e.g., Naglieri & Das, 1997b), it is assumed that an optimum level of performance in each processing domain is necessary for effective and efficient learning and problem solving. In addition, a deficiency in one or more of the PASS processes will impede acquisition of knowledge and disrupt cognitive activity as well (Naglieri & Das, 1997c). Also, some tasks are more dependent on one PASS process than another.

Most learning and problem-solving activities depend on more than one PASS process. Reading, for example, requires Simultaneous processing in recognizing words and comprehending what is read, and Successive processing in decoding syntax. Attention is required in maintaining an appropriate level of concentration, and Planning is needed in determining how much or little is read and whether the reader can skip sections without missing vital information. It is not unusual, however, for an activity to require more of one PASS process than another. It is also likely that the same activity can be solved, and the same results obtained, by using the various processes in different ways.

High and Low Scores

A high score on one of the PASS processes may indicate how a person will deal with a certain learning or problem-solving situation, thus suggesting a learning preference. Consider the following children.

Ten-year-old Jake performed extremely well on the Successive domain on the CAS and well above average for his age on Planning, Attention, and Simultaneous. He is a quick learner, especially when he has to listen carefully to the teacher's instructions and explanations. When watching Jake in class, you can almost hear him saying to himself, "Do this first, now this, now this—right, that's the way it goes—now this, and this." He's quick to remind others what they have to do. In a small group exercise, for example, Jake will tell the other children all the teacher's directions in exactly the right sequence. At home, Jake is learning the piano and his mother tells about how he easily remembers tunes and then can "pick" them out on the keyboard after just one "hearing."

Fourteen-year old Tracy has a very high Planning score and also a high Attention score. She doesn't miss very much going on around her. As you would expect, when you give Tracy something to do that is creative, she can come up with a number of alternatives and then go about the process of deciding which is the best way to achieve her goal. Unlike many of her school friends, she loves puzzles and mind games and can spend hours working through puzzle books.

Jake and Tracy don't always do better than their classmates on projects or exams, even though both are in the top 20% of the students in their grade. What is apparent from spending time with each of them is their preferred way of doing things. Jake is good when information is presented orally (sequentially), but he also does things very methodically, one at a time. Tracy likes to check things out before she begins and does a lot of self-monitoring to make sure she's "on the right track."

> Dan is also 14 years old. His CAS profile shows that he is above average on Planning, Attention, and Successive processing but has a very high Simultaneous score. His teacher talks about Dan as being a good conceptualizer. Things seem to fall into place for him. In contrast to Jake, who does very well with information presented in sequential fashion (often orally), seeing Dan in class reminds you of a photographer taking in everything he's watching; not surprisingly, he has a good visual memory. He has a vivid imagination, likes many genres of books including fantasy, detective stories, and nonfiction, and has a very good general knowledge for a person of his age. Dan admits, "I like looking at things. I'm not a very good listener."

Each of these children appears to have a preferred way of learning and solving problems. The CAS tells about their strengths, and this may help the teacher to present ideas and information in a way that will benefit each child. For example, the teacher might support Jake's strength by saying, "OK, Jake, here's a list of the things you'll need to solve the problem." Alternatively, the teacher might emphasize the characteristics of the activity if it doesn't involve a successive strategy: "Jake, you need to make sure you organize the whole task into steps before getting started."

Students who have a cognitive or relative weakness in one or more of the PASS processes are likely to demonstrate a problem in a number of teaching-learning situations. Additionally, they may have a preference to use one of the PASS processes not for efficiency, but for compensation.

> Eight-year-old Charity has an average Simultaneous score and a depressed Successive score but has not fallen behind her classmates in schoolwork. Her teacher reports that Charity is a little slow to pick up new ideas but assumes that it is because she is easily distracted. Because

Charity doesn't read very well, the teacher spends a little more time with her, one-to-one, especially when the class is involved in group work. She also has organized some home reading activities with which the parents can help every other night. The teacher finds that making sure Charity writes down instructions accurately during the lesson, especially when they are given orally, helps her to stay on task.

Mike is 12 years old. He has average to good Simultaneous and Successive scores but a depressed Planning score and a much lower Attention score. He often doesn't get much work done during class. Watching him operate (and *operate* is the best term to use) would be amusing if it wasn't to the detriment of his school achievement. He is a youngster with a quick wit and seems interested in just about everything other than what he's supposed to be doing. Most often, he doesn't complete the exercises assigned by the teacher because he misses the detail or the instructions given because he is not paying attention. When the teacher explains what he should be doing, Mike has no problem understanding.

Children with a PASS weakness or weaknesses are likely to attract the attention of a teacher and eventually the school psychologist, especially when cognitive deficiencies are reflected in low achievement. Knowing the child's cognitive profile is of greatest value when the teacher is aware of the problem and knows how to capitalize on a child's strengths or focus specifically on strengthening a deficit.

THE INSTRUCTIONAL CYCLE

For teaching and learning to be efficient, the process must be systematic to the extent that what is to be learned, how it will be taught, and how learning will be evaluated must be clearly defined and understood. This is often described as a cycle including four phases: Assessment, Preparation, Instruction, and Evaluation.

Assessment

The initial evaluation of the child may involve formal or informal, norm-referenced or criterion-referenced assessments of achievement; review of the student's learning over time; and consultation with relevant stakeholders including the student, other teachers, a counselor, and parents. Norm-referenced tests of reading, mathematics, general knowledge, science, and other areas provide useful information about the relative achievement of the learner when compared to peers. Criterion-referenced tests—sometimes called curriculum-based assessment—are useful for identifying a student's performance in curriculum areas; on these measures students are assessed only against their personal mastery of the content and not against other students. The test results can guide instruction on a specific aspect of the curriculum or a learning process, can be linked directly to teaching and evaluation of performance, and can help students evaluate their own performance when working through an aspect of the curriculum.

Preparation

This phase of the instructional cycle includes the selection of content, teaching methods, and resources. In determining the content to be taught, it is important to have a clear understanding of the desired learning outcome. Preparation also involves selecting teaching methods and materials. When preparing for teaching, the instructor should make decisions about how to address a PASS processing weakness. The instructor might decide to focus on developing the deficient process or ignore it and work on the learner's processing strength. The former situation is illustrated below for working with an Attention difficulty:

> Trevor is 12 years old. His CAS profile shows depressed PASS scores generally (he has been identified as having mild mental retardation). An Individual Education Plan (IEP) has been written for him, and the classroom teacher and school psychologist decided to focus on improving Trevor's attending behavior as a starting point. This was thought to be appropriate, as the boy's failure to pay attention when instructions are being given means that he can't begin any lesson activity because he doesn't have the information he needs. The teacher uses a standard phrase, "All right, listen now," before she gives any instruction; she waits until Trevor is paying attention to her. Trevor also has a prompt on the corner of his desk that reads "Stop. Think about what I'm doing. Do it."

> # DON'T FORGET
> ## Selected Processing Dimensions of Reading
>
> **Successive**
>
> - performing phonetic analysis to break down the word into the sequence of sounds
> - holding the sound sequence in working memory
> - children low in Successive may use a Simultaneous approach
>
> **Simultaneous**
>
> - recognizing the patterns of letters and sounds
> - noting the correspondence of the pattern of letters and pattern of sounds
> - seeing the word as a whole
> - children low in Simultaneous may use a Successive approach
>
> *Note.* From Kirby and Williams (1991).

Instruction

This phase relates directly to the decisions made during the preparation phase. Teaching may follow a prescriptive sequence of teaching, testing, teaching, and testing. This may involve modeling the desired behavior, practicing skills, and then monitoring progress.

Evaluation

Evaluation may occur at three levels in an instructional cycle: it may be included (a) during instruction to direct later programming decisions (called formative assessment), (b) at the completion of a unit of work (summative assessment), or (c) after the program of instruction/intervention has been completed (meta-evaluation). Evaluation may involve descriptions of performance and outcomes, as well as the ongoing collection of samples of students' work such as essays, projects, worksheets, or other devices that measure outcomes or achievements. Although the emphasis at this point may be on acquisition of academic content, evaluation of the child's use of PASS

≡ Rapid Reference

Contemporary approaches to teaching and learning have been subsumed under the label *cognitive education,* which reflects the importance of thinking skills in teaching and learning (see Ashman & Conway, 1997). These authors employ a number of principles that emphasize the active involvement of the learner. Among them are the following:

- learning that occurs within a curriculum context rather than learning in isolation
- instruction and learning experience that are integrated and balanced
- instruction that occurs as a continually recurring process in which learning of new information or skills builds on previously learned information or skills
- mediation by teachers and others that assists the learner to focus on relevant aspects of the process
- instructional routines and "think aloud" methods to provide models of strategic thought
- scaffolding that helps the learner take control of the teaching-learning process
- peer-mediated learning to motivate and assist students in gaining insights into others' problem-solving behavior
- immediate feedback so the learner can make adjustments as needed

processes is also important. The meta-evaluation cycle should be accomplished with the administration of formal tests, using the method described in Chapter 4 of this book and with consideration of the points listed in Rapid Reference above.

GENERAL PRINCIPLES FOR INTERVENTION AND REMEDIATION

Learning is a complex process that involves linking new knowledge with information already held in memory through the application and use of PASS processes. This view of learning is consistent with many cognitive education approaches that might occur in a remediation setting. It includes four important steps:

1. Learning must take place through observation. A first step is to know what the goal of the activity is. If a student has a processing deficit, it is essential to demonstrate each of the steps in the learning activity.

2. Learning must include practice—providing students with experience in using the new skills and knowledge, giving them the chance to make errors, modifying behavior, and testing boundaries. It is rarely sufficient simply to tell a child about a concept or a learning or problem-solving process.

3. Learning must involve the application of principles. This might entail following a set of steps (e.g., directions to construct a model aircraft), following rules (e.g., using "i" before "e" except after "c" when spelling), or following a procedure (e.g., "Stop, think, do, check").

4. Learning must involve generalization. Generalization can involve the simple adaptation of principles or the process of creativity that includes looking for alternative ways of solving problems.

In applying various instructional methods to meet the needs of a child with a PASS weakness, the primary goal is to improve the child's academic performance through instruction that takes into account the nature of the child's cognitive weakness. Options include instructing better use of the weak processing area and changing the processing requirements of the task to better accommodate the child's PASS profile. These methods are summarized in Figure 7.1 and are more fully described in the remainder of this chapter.

TEACHING THE USE OF PLANNING PROCESSES THROUGH PROCESS-BASED INSTRUCTION AND PLANNING FACILITATION

Ashman and Conway (1993) developed a method called Process-Based Instruction (PBI) that is relevant to this discussion for several reasons, perhaps mostly because both PBI and the CAS share a common theoretical framework: Luria's functional organization of the brain. The PBI method, however, puts emphasis on planning as a fundamental process that every individual must develop during the course of his or her life. PBI takes advan-

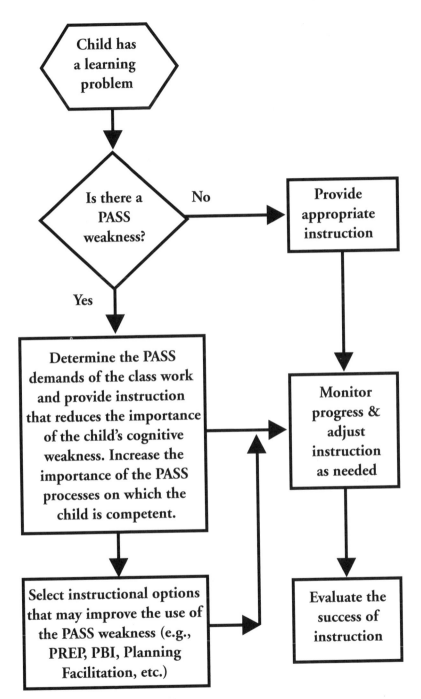

Figure 7.1 Intervention Flow Chart

tage of the many classroom activities, projects, and learning events that can be oriented toward planning, to introduce the concept in a systematic way. Because the intent of PBI is to teach children to better use planning processes, it should be applied when the goal is to increase children's knowledge and application of the process.

Ashman and Conway (1989, 1993) developed PBI as a way of teaching students how to learn and how to solve problems. The PBI model is a four-phase process—one that encompasses the learning of specific skills and information *and* the learning of general planning and monitoring procedures that apply in most, if not all, learning contexts. In each of the four phases, three teaching-learning procedures are employed (orientation, acquisition, and application) to ensure that new information and/or skills are assimilated by learners into their existing knowledge bases. The model provides freedom for teachers to personalize the use of planning in their own and their students' teaching and learning activities.

Phases of the PBI Model

Introduction.   This phase involves students' initial contact with PBI. The main focus of the phase is to provide students with their first formal experience of a PBI plan for a specific curriculum task. Students may be introduced to plans prepared by the teacher or to those prepared jointly by the teacher and students, either before or after attempting the task. Some plans are generated by the students themselves individually or in a small group, before or after attempting the task.

Establishment.   Once students have used plans for specific curriculum tasks, it is important that they appreciate that plans can be applied in a range of situations within the same curriculum area. The crucial feature of the establishment phase is ensuring that the teacher and students adapt plans for related tasks, thereby demonstrating the application of plans rather than depending on many individual plans each time a new task is presented. Students (or indeed, the teacher) must not become reliant on any one plan.

Consolidation.   The consolidation phase allows students and teachers to see that plans have a broader role in learning and problem solving than the single application to a specific task. Students are encouraged to identify tasks in other curriculum areas whereby an amendment to the plan will assist in achieving

DON'T FORGET

It is important to teach strategies that develop the students' independence in learning and problem solving and maximize their use of cognitive processes. This means ensuring that the teaching-learning process:

1. supports content and process learning.
2. provides examples or models that make learning easy.
3. provides support in the early phases of learning that can be withdrawn progressively to enable the learner to become independent.

the goal. As students become familiar with the use of plans, they also learn to abbreviate (as the steps become automated) and link them with other plans if a task involves a procedure of two (or more) stages.

Incorporation. Once a student has a clear understanding of the use of plans for a number of applications, he or she becomes more adept at making judgments about what actions or decisions are needed to deal with situations. Students draw on (a) their knowledge of how to develop, use, and adapt both specific and general plans according to the circumstances, (b) an understanding of the constellation of learning and problem events that are appropriate at their particular developmental level, and (c) their ability to anticipate where planning success or failure may occur.

PBI Plans

An example of a teacher-made plan for use with a class of 10-year-olds is shown in Table 7.2. Notice that it contains a series of sentences that are sequenced and include a cueing step (Step 1), an acting step (Step 2), a monitoring step (Step 3), possibly another acting step (Step 4), a second monitoring step (Step 5), and a verifying step (Step 6). Notice that plans must be written in the student's own language. This characteristic of PBI sets it apart from other cognitive education approaches. Note that the plan says "I" and "my," not "you" and "your." Through this process, students gain a sense of ownership of the plan as they record it in their own words. Numerous examples of plans are given in Ashman and Conway (1993).

Plans for Attention and Simultaneous and Successive Processing

There are no prescribed methods for making and using plans. Teachers are free to integrate plan development into regular classroom practice in any way that

Table 7.2 A Plan for Writing a Paragraph

Step 1.	What is the paragraph about?
Step 2.	Write sentences.
Step 3.	Have I said what I want?
Step 4.	Revise sentences if needed.
Step 5.	Does the paragraph make sense?
Step 6.	Share my work.

supports their personal teaching style. They must decide, however, if a plan is needed for a particular classroom activity and, if so, how the planning process can best be incorporated into the lesson or learning experience. The familiarity of the students with PBI, their level of academic achievement, and the teacher's desired level of control over classroom routines affect the choice.

Although the philosophy PBI encourages is one of full inclusion and regular class teaching and learning, it has been used in diverse instructional settings. It has been applied to all curriculum areas, from preschool to senior high school, and in whole class and remedial, one-to-one settings. The focus has always been on teaching students to become independent thinkers and decision-makers through the systematic introduction of Planning. However, it has wider applicability. For example, plans can be developed to highlight other PASS processes of Attention and Simultaneous and Successive processing while maintaining the general benefit of showing students how to take control of their own learning and problem solving.

Trevor's situation (see page 157) provides an example of how plans can be adapted to focus on Attention and Simultaneous and Successive processing. Recall that the boy has mild mental retardation and a CAS result showing low standard scores across the profile. The teacher uses PBI regularly in her class, and all the children have experience using plans. After getting the rest of the class to work on their writing activity, she sits with Trevor to amend his plan so that it emphasizes on-task behavior (Table 7.3). The plan has not changed much from the original (Table 7.2), except that it prompts Trevor recall what he is supposed to be doing. She talks through the plan so that he knows exactly what it is asking him to do. Every few minutes she checks back to make sure he is working and is surprised, and encouraged, to find that he has fin-

Table 7.3 A Plan to Focus on Attention

Step 1.	What am I supposed to be doing?
Step 2.	Write sentences.
Step 3.	Have I written enough?
Step 4.	Add more if not.
Step 5.	Check that I've done what I'm supposed to; if not, add more.
Step 6.	Read my work. Is it OK?
Step 7.	Share my work.

ished the exercise at the same time as many of his peers—although not quite to the same degree of sophistication. Examples of plans that emphasize Successive and Simultaneous processes are given in Tables 7.4 and 7.5.

One significant advantage of PBI is its adaptability to the needs of the teacher and students at any given time. Because the teacher and students create plans to serve a specific purpose, PBI has almost unlimited applications. However, it is not the only application that can support CAS assessments. There are a number of remedial programs that focus on PASS processes. These are discussed below.

Table 7.4 A Plan to Focus on Successive Processing

Step 1.	What happened second in the story?
Step 2.	Write sentences.
Step 3.	Do they tell the story from start to finish?
Step 4.	Change the order if needed.
Step 5.	Does the order now make sense?
Step 6.	Share my work.

Facilitating the Planning Process

The relationship between planning and instruction has been closely examined in a series of papers beginning with Cormier, Carlson, and Das (1990) and

Table 7.5 A Plan to Focus on Simultaneous Processing

Step 1.	What do I want to tell about the character?
Step 2.	Write sentences.
Step 3.	Does each sentence tell something new about the character?
Step 4.	Add or change information if needed.
Step 5.	Does the story tell everything I want about the character?
Step 6.	Share my work.

Kar, Dash, Das, and Carlson (1992). These researchers developed a method that stimulated children's use of planning and had positive effects on performance. The method was based on the assumption that a student's use of planning processes should be facilitated rather than directly instructed, and that a student should discover the value of strategies without being specifically told to. This is quite different from the approach adopted in PBI in which instruction about the planning process is made explicit. Nevertheless, the results of the two studies demonstrate that the method has utility.

Both Cormier and colleagues (1990) and Kar and associates (1992) demonstrated that students differentially benefit from a verbalization technique intended to facilitate planning. They found that participants who initially performed poorly on measures of planning earned significantly higher scores than those with good scores in planning. The verbalization technique facilitated planning and an organized examination of the demands of the activity and analysis of the relevant information for those who needed to do this the most (those with low planning scores). The studies were the basis for two applied investigations by Naglieri and Gottling (1995, 1997) involving math calculation. Both studies demonstrated that an intervention designed to facilitate the use of planning helped those with low scores in planning, but minimal improvement was found on multiplication problems for those with high planning scores. This study was the first to examine the usefulness of facilitation of planning as part of mathematics instruction for learning disabled students. Because the results suggested that students benefited differentially from the instruction based on their cognitive processing scores, matching the instruction to the cognitive weakness of the student was shown to be important.

The investigators worked with a sample of elementary school students who attended an independent school that specialized in the treatment of students with significant learning problems who had made minimal educational progress in public special education programs. Two teachers provided instruction to the students on a regular basis; during the study, the investigators consulted with the teachers on a weekly basis to assist in the application of the intervention, monitor the progress of the students, and consider ways of facilitating classroom discussions. Students completed mathematics work sheets in a sequence of 7 baseline and 21 intervention sessions over about a 2-month period.

In the intervention phase, there was a 10-minute period for completing a mathematics page, a 10-minute period for facilitating planning, and another 10-minute period for mathematics. All students were exposed to the intervention sessions that involved the three 10-minute segments of mathematics/discussion/mathematics in 30-minute instructional periods. During the group discussion, self-reflection and discussion were facilitated so that the children would understand the need to plan and use an efficient strategy when completing the mathematics problems. Probes were presented by the teachers to facilitate discussion that would encourage the children to consider ways to be more successful. When a student provided a response, this often became the beginning point for discussion and further development of the idea. Probes illustrative of those used by the teachers are listed in Rapid Reference on page 168. The teachers made no direct statements such as "That is correct" or "Remember to use that same strategy," nor did they provide feedback on the number correct; and they never gave mathematics instruction. The role of the teacher was to facilitate self-reflection and, therefore, encourage students to plan so that they could complete the worksheets.

Both the low- and high-scoring groups differentially benefited from the instruction even though both groups had similar initial baseline scores in math computation; students who were low in planning improved consistently across the three intervention segments (113%). Students with high planning scores also improved, but the improvement was about 50% less than that seen for students with low planning scores.

This study was replicated and extended in an investigation by Naglieri and Johnson (in press) using the same procedures as those used by Naglieri and Gottling (1995, 1997), but with a larger sample and with children with learn-

≡ Rapid Reference

Probes used by teachers in the mathematics and planning study:

- Can anyone tell me anything about these problems?
- Let's talk about how you did the worksheet.
- Why did you do it that way?
- How did you do the problems?
- What could you have done to get more correct?
- What did it teach you?
- What else did you notice about how this page was done?
- What will you do next time?
- I noticed that many of you did not do what you said was important. What do you think of that?

In response to these probes, the students made comments such as:

- I'll do all the easy ones first.
- I do them row by row.
- When I get distracted, I'll move my seat.
- I have to remember to borrow.
- I do the ones with 1s, 0s and 10s in them—they're easy.
- If it's a big problem [all big numbers on the top] you don't have to borrow, so do it first.
- Be sure to get them right, not just get them done.
- I have to stay awake.
- I have to remember to add the numbers after multiplying.
- I have to keep the columns straight.

ing problems. Because the purpose of Naglieri and Johnson's study was to determine if children with specific PASS profiles would show different rates of improvement, children were selected to form groups based on their CAS scores. Children with a cognitive weakness (see Chapter 4) in Planning, Attention, Simultaneous, and Successive scales were selected to form contrast groups. The contrasting groups of children responded very differently to the intervention.

As summarized in Table 7.6, the four groups of children in Naglieri and

Table 7.6 Percentage of Improvement Over Baseline Rates for Children With Cognitive Weaknesses on the CAS

	P	A	Sm	Sc	Percentage of Change
CW in Planning	70	86	89	92	142
CW in Simultaneous	93	90	70	90	−11
CW in Attention	87	71	93	102	50
CW in Successive	88	103	88	72	39

Note. CW = cognitive weakness as defined in Chapter 4 of this book.

Johnson's study were quite different. The PASS profiles clearly show a cognitive weakness in only one of the four scales. Examination of responsiveness to treatment shows that these groups of children did not benefit equally from the group instruction. The children with a weakness in Planning improved considerably (about 140%) over baseline, whereas the children with a weakness in the other processes improved considerably less. Thus the treatment validity of the PASS processes is again demonstrated.

Naglieri and Johnson (in press) demonstrated that teachers can easily apply this intervention to assist children who are poor in math calculation and have a weakness in planning. Teachers should use the Planning Facilitation Intervention procedure described in Rapid Reference on page 170.

Children with a weakness in Planning on the CAS will improve the most if the method described here is followed. Additional work on math skills may follow once the processing limitation has been addressed. If, however, the child does not have a Planning weakness, consideration should be given to identifying difficulties with the other processes and linking instruction directly to the remediation of math skills.

In the PBI and Planning Facilitation methods, the teacher's task is to develop the students' knowledge of how to generate, use, and adapt plans as circumstances demand; assist students' understanding of problem-solving methods appropriate to the particular developmental level; and encourage students to anticipate when planning strategies may or may not be effective. Ashman and Conway's approach is very direct, whereas Planning Facilitation is indirect. Both methods have been shown to be effective. PBI provides a means

≡ Rapid Reference

Planning Facilitation Intervention

Intervention Step 1: The teacher gives each child a worksheet and says, "Here is another math worksheet for you to do. Please try to get as many of the problems correct as you can. You will have 10 minutes." Slight variations on this instruction are permitted, but do not give any additional information.

Intervention Step 2: This step requires that the teacher facilitate a discussion that probes the children regarding how they completed the worksheet and how they will go about completing worksheets in the future. Teachers do not attempt to reinforce the children. For example, if a child says "I used xyz strategy" the teacher should not say "Good, and be sure to do that next time." Instead the teacher may probe, saying "And did that work for you?" or a similar statement that encourages the child to consider the effectiveness of the strategy. The general goals are to encourage the children to:

- describe how they did the worksheet;
- verbalize ideas (this facilitates planning);
- explain why some methods work better than others;
- interact actively with the teacher;
- be self-reflective;
- think about what they will do the next time they get a worksheet.

Intervention Step 3: The teacher gives each child a worksheet and says, "Here is another math worksheet for you to do. Please try to get as many of the problems correct as you can. You will have 10 minutes." Slight variations on this instruction are permitted, but do not give any additional information.

Aids to Facilitate Discussion:

- Make an overhead of a blank worksheet so the children can see it during discussion.
- Make an overhead of a completed worksheet (with the name omitted).
- Do a blank worksheet as a group on the overhead.

Note. Adapted from Naglieri and Gottling (1997).

of encouraging planning within regular classroom activities, but it can also be used in small group and remediation settings. Ashman and Conway's (1993) work emphasized PBI as a teaching framework, and more recent studies (e.g., Hay, in press) have shown PBI to be valuable in changing students' and teachers' behavior in elementary and secondary classrooms. In relation to the approaches used by Cormier and colleagues (1990), Naglieri's studies encourage the application of methods that attempt to facilitate the use of planning in the classroom. The results of targeted instruction to smaller groups of individuals with low scores in planning may still be accomplished through PBI.

IMPROVING READING THROUGH THE PASS REMEDIAL PROGRAM (PREP)

The PASS Remedial Program (PREP; Das, in press), the CAS, and PBI derive from the same information processing model of A. R. Luria. PREP aims at improving the Simultaneous and Successive processing that underlie reading, while at the same time avoiding the direct teaching of word reading skills. When a young child fails to learn how to read, it is largely due to a deficit in Successive processing, which is the process that helps the child to sequence different items or letters and words. For example, a child cannot read *friend* or *tongue* if remembering the sequence of letters in each word and converting them to spoken words is problematic. Difficulties in Successive processing may cause difficulties in acquiring and/or using phonological coding. This, in turn, may lead to an inability to decode words effectively, which ultimately leads to reading failure.

Poor performance in either Simultaneous or Successive processing may be due to (a) a decreased ability to use the process, (b) barriers to the use of the process that can be overcome by training, or (c) an inclination not to use the process when it is optimal. It is important to re-emphasize, however, that no cognitive task requires one process alone. It is a matter of emphasis. A child may use either coding process, depending on the task requirements (e.g., the use of Successive processing in spelling or decoding words phonetically) or the child's habitual mode of information processing. PREP provides (a) alternatives for children who cannot use the processes effectively, (b) experience and practice in one or both processes, and (c) specific training to help the child recognize the most efficient approach to use when reading. Therefore PREP is structured so that students use Simultaneous or Successive processes in task-appropriate ways. Attention and Planning are also considered, as Attention is required in performing each task, and Planning is encouraged through discussions during and following the children's attempts at each activity.

Like PBI, there is an emphasis on strategies that help coding and decoding, monitoring of performance, prediction, and specific reading activities such as sounding and sound blending. Rather than being taught strategies by the tutor, children are encouraged to become aware of their use of strategies through verbalization.

PREP consists of 10 tasks that vary considerably in content and requirements. It employs two types of training materials: those that are described as "global" (which foster the use of Successive or Simultaneous processes) and "bridging" (which help the student extend a particular strategy to an academic task such as word identification). The global process training tasks teach students to use and internalize reading strategies. These activities maximize generalization and facilitate transfer of learning. The bridging process provides training in strategies that relate specifically to reading and spelling. These two parts of PREP encourage the application of strategies to academic tasks through verbal mediation and internalization processes.

PREP is a flexible program to the extent that the tasks can be administered in any order. However, it is important to consider the student's strengths and weaknesses based on CAS assessment. For a student who is experiencing only Simultaneous processing difficulties, only those tasks with a simultaneous focus need be included. Alternatively, for younger students who are primarily experiencing decoding difficulties in reading, the use of only the Successive tasks may be appropriate.

The global component of a task is always followed by its paired bridging component. For most students the program should begin with Level 1 for all selected tasks, and individual adjustments can then be made as necessary. Beginning with Level 1 ensures that most students meet with success from the outset of the program. It is also important to avoid spending too much time on any one task or specific skill, as this may lead to overlearning, which inhibits transfer of learning (Das, Naglieri, & Kirby, 1994). An example of two global PREP activities is given in Rapid Reference on page 173.

Practical Applications of PREP

PREP is most effective when a teacher is working with 2 to 10 students. A manual has been prepared to assist teachers for this purpose. Although the same amount of remedial guidance cannot be easily provided in a large group

≡ Rapid Reference

Two PREP Activities

Joining Shapes: Successive

- Have children work in pairs.
- Provide each child with a copy of the sample response sheet (contains shapes displayed in rows of three only).
- As a class, review the four rules for drawing the pattern.
- Use the PREP instructions for Difficulty Level 1.
- Monitor the children's performance following each connection (once they understand the task requirements, they can monitor each other's performance).
- In pairs, have the children compare their completed patterns and discuss strategies used for remembering the instructions.

Sentence Verification: Simultaneous

The instructions in the PREP manual can be used as guidelines for introducing this task.

- Display groups of photos (Items 1 to 5 from the global task) on a storyboard or chalkboard.
- Read the passage or sentence that corresponds to the group of photos.
- Encourage the children to find the picture that matches what you read. Always ask them to explain why they chose a particular picture.
- Note that other photos or pictures from magazines and corresponding sentences can also be used for this activity.

Note. From Das and Kendrick (1997).

of students, the results of extending PREP to larger groups have been positive. However, a caution is needed: As the number of students extends beyond two or three, some children may fail to gain from PREP. Guidelines for the effective application of PREP are given in Das and Kendrick (1997).

PREP has been tested in a number of studies reported in Das and Kendrick (1997). The program was used by Carlson and Das (1997) with underachieving students in Chapter 1 programs in California. These students received two 50-minute PREP sessions per week for 3 months. The students who received remediation gained significantly in word identification and word attack skills. Work in the school over 5 years has shown consistent improvement in reading skills of underachieving children. Another study by Das, Mishra, and Pool (1995) with a group of over 50 fourth grade students in Edmonton, Canada, showed that the PREP group improved significantly on word identification and word attack skills. In a second phase of the study, the children who had previously been in the control group were given either the global part or the bridging part of PREP for the same length of time without changing their overall reading competence.

A Spanish adaptation of PREP has been prepared at the University of Zaragoza, and another has been developed for use in private and government schools in South Africa. Thus, PREP is being applied to children from a wide variety of cultural and economic backgrounds.

PASS AND LEARNING PROBLEMS: A THEORETICAL APPROACH TO INTERVENTION

In *Learning Problems: A Cognitive Approach*, Kirby and Williams (1991) suggest that the PASS theory is an appropriate framework for understanding learning difficulties and identifying methods to address them. The book is based on the view that teachers who are aware of the relationships between PASS processes and academic performance, as well as the individual child's PASS strengths and weaknesses, will be better able to help them succeed.

Kirby and Williams provide several chapters on the diagnosis and remediation of learning problems and an excellent discussion of the classroom symptoms of PASS problems. These guidelines for evaluation of the child's classroom performance, when coupled with results from the CAS, can provide a thorough view of the child's status. See Rapid Reference on page 175 for examples. Kirby and Williams suggest that if a student cannot use the processes very well, alternative ways to solve the task should be considered. That is, the task should be taught in a way that puts emphasis on a different PASS process (see the section Selecting Academic Tasks That Fit the Child below). If a process has not been developed, experience and practice are provided (as discussed above for PBI, PREP, and Planning Facilitation and in sections below). If a student has not used a process when it is most efficient, specific training in recognizing the appropriate use should be implemented (PBI and PREP also do this).

≡ Rapid Reference

Classroom Problems Related to PASS Processes

Planning

1. Failure to switch strategies according to the demands of the task
2. Failure to correct misinterpretation of what is read
3. Inconsistent application of spelling or math rules when solving problems
4. Disorganized completion of assignments
5. Failure to devise or use aids when completing work

Simultaneous

1. Failure to recognize sight words quickly
2. Failure to interpret word, sentence, or passage meaning
3. Difficulty seeing the shapes of words or working with spatial tasks
4. Failure to see patterns in text or math problems
5. Failure to comprehend math word problems

Attention

1. Limited span of attention
2. Failure to focus on relevant aspects of assignments
3. Difficulty in resisting distractions in the classroom
4. Incomplete assignments
5. Tendency to answer questions based on incomplete information

Successive

1. Poor word decoding skills
2. Failure to comprehend syntax structure
3. Failure to pronounce words and sequence word segments accurately
4. Difficulty in following steps, or omitting steps needed to solve problems
5. Lack of comprehension of the sequence of events in a story

Note. From Kirby and Williams (1991).

Teaching Use of the PASS Processes

Planning

Kirby and Williams (1991) suggest that if a child is weak in planning, it is reasonable for the teacher to teach students how to plan. They suggest that the teacher begin with a task that involves planning and identify the part where the student experiences difficulty, then teach at that point with simplified content. The goal is to (a) improve general planning in less complex content, and (b) then move to academic content. It is the teacher's task to assess what strategies the student uses, expose the student to a situation in which alternative strategies are needed, and then provide the student with new strategies. Instruction may involve modeling, explicit verbal instruction, self-instruction, self-monitoring, or a combination of these methods. For example, a general visual and phonic analysis strategy should be used first in word identification followed by the use of context. Strategies such as analyzing syntax and semantics should be used at the sentence comprehension level, and other strategies to extract main ideas and summarizing should be used at the paragraph level. It is important to note that PBI attempts to teach planning and involves many of the suggestions made by Kirby and Williams in a systematic and progressive way.

Simultaneous

Simultaneous processing can be improved by teaching children to recognize that concepts in reading, spelling, and math can be organized into groups—for example, the theme of written text, or patterns in the sequence of letters or numbers. Working with patterns of shapes and knowledge of conceptual organization (e.g., of people, places, things) may also be important.

Attention

When an attentional processing problem is identified, Kirby and Williams (1991) suggest that a cognitive control program be used. This method is a blend of cognitive and behavior therapy that leads to behavior change through self-instruction. Speech is an important mechanism of change. The essence of the technique involves instructing students in a set of verbal methods that they can use to control their own behavior. This not only encourages the students to be independent but also facilitates internalization of the methods to increase attention.

Successive

Children's performance on tasks that involve successive processing may be augmented by attending to three components: the child's knowledge base; span of memory; and application of strategies that assist in sequencing objects, ideas, and events. Because poor basic skills can interfere with adequate performance, the information needed to solve problems must be provided. For example, to facilitate spelling the teacher might give the child a group of letters (e.g., E-L-I-T-S-E-O-I-N-V) and instruct the child to use those letters to make the word *television*. Children's memory span can be enhanced by teaching them to use strategies that facilitate recall (see, e.g., Mastropieri & Schruggs, 1991).

Kirby and Williams provide many examples of working with PASS processes. They also make clear that they believe processing problems seldom exist in isolation and that classroom activities and instruction often involve the use of several PASS processes. Finally, they recognize that deficient background knowledge often coexists with PASS processing difficulties and that each area may need to be addressed in different ways to obtain significant changes in academic performance.

Selecting Academic Tasks That Fit the Child

When a child has a specific processing deficit, the teacher has two options: first, to train the cognitive weakness; and, second, to reconstruct the task so that the learner can use a processing strength to achieve success. Thus the teacher can alter the processing demands of schoolwork by selecting alternative methods that fit the child's PASS characteristics. For example, a child with a successive processing weakness can be taught math facts in a way that puts most emphasis on that process (e.g., an oral drill and practice method that requires the child to say the fact in the same sequence many times: $7 + 8 = 15$). If the child is taught to use strategies to solve math facts (e.g., $7 + 8 = 7 + 7 + 1$), then the task relies more on planning and less on successive processes. Thus, with all other teaching-learning aspects remaining the same, this alternative approach allows the child to function more effectively than before by circumventing the successive processing problem and increasing the importance of planning.

This approach reduces the demands of the process with which the child has the most difficulty. That is, if a child is weak in simultaneous processing, instructional materials should teach the use of a strategy (Planning) that facilitates good processing. For example, if a child is weak in reading comprehension and weak in simultaneous processing, the teacher should consider using a story mapping method (Idol,

1987). This method helps the reader see how information in a story is interrelated and draws attention to the common elements of the text (see also Pressley & Woloshyn, 1995).

The story map is a diagrammatic representation of text (see Figure 7.2) that shows the relationships among the parts of the story (simultaneous). The story map also includes activities that are conducted after initial introduction to the task and, most important, a group of probes to facilitate performance. For example, the teacher is encouraged to have the children underline and label parts of the text, create their own story maps, and ask themselves questions about the text. To do so, probes are provided such as "How did you complete the story map?" "What is a good way to remember the parts of the story?" and "What did this teach you?" This engages the planning process (see the section Planning Facilitation earlier in this chapter), whereas the story map itself involves simultaneous processes.

The story map method can also be used as an initial plan with children who have learning disabilities in written language. These students often write stories that are disorganized, incomplete, and disconnected (Scheid, 1993). Using the story map as an initial step prior to producing the written document may assist in organization of the goals and parts of the text (like a PBI plan).

If the child is weak in successive processing and has problems remembering order, strategies (plans) that organize the material differently (involving simultaneous processes) should be considered. There are many examples of helping students to remember facts provided by Mastropieri and Schruggs (1991). For example, if a child has difficulty remembering the order of mathematical operations, the saying "My Dear Aunt Sally" is taught to remind the

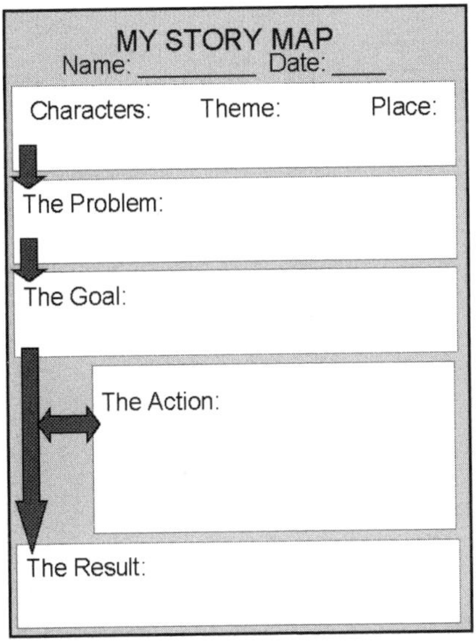

MY STORY MAP
Name: _____ Date: ____

| Characters: | Theme: | Place: |

The Problem:

The Goal:

The Action:

The Result:

Figure 7.2 Story Map Example of Using PASS Processes as a Guide to Selection of Instructional Materials

Note. Adapted from Pressley and Woloshyn (1995).

child to Multiply, Divide, Add, and then Subtract. This strategy reduces the importance of successive processing and increases the role of planning and simultaneous processes in the task.

Each approach described above can be effective in remediating the learning problems experienced by children and adults. Each has advantages and disadvantages; these depend on the context in which teaching-learning and remediation is to occur. The aim is to find an instructional method that satisfies the learner's needs, encourages gains in a deficit process, and facilitates learning and problem solving through existing processing strengths. To accomplish this the teacher and school psychologist must do two things: first, evaluate the current requirements of the academic tasks with which the child is having difficulty; second, determine how the task can be amended to maximize the use of PASS processes.

The first step in examining the PASS processing demands of a task requires a working knowledge of the theory. This can be obtained by reading of Chapter 1 of this text and relevant sections of Naglieri and Das (1997c) and Das, Naglieri, and Kirby (1994). The second step is to identify aspects of the curriculum that do not place a burden on the child's cognitive weakness. To do so, practitioners should collaborate closely with the teacher to select the best materials and teaching strategies for the individual child.

CONCLUSIONS

There are a number of ways in which the school psychologist and a classroom teacher can use the information obtained from the CAS to develop general instruction and remediation procedures for students at various grade levels. If one accepts that the primary responsibility of education practitioners is to provide opportunities to maximize the learning outcomes for students, then there is a concomitant responsibility to seek new technologies that lead toward that goal. The PASS theory and CAS provide a mechanism for achieving this objective because they direct attention toward students' processing strengths and weakness, which can then be addressed by innovative teaching-learning methods.

> **DON'T FORGET**
> ....
> There are few "quick fixes" in education. If a student of average ability is having problems, it may be that the prerequisite knowledge is missing or the student does not have a range of learning and problem-solving strategies available to deal with the task(s) being presented, or any other combination of learner, teacher, setting, and curriculum interactions.

It is important to stress that there is no single "right" way to teach a child. To a large extent, educators must try a number of alternatives to match their teaching method with the student's preferred approach to learning. In addition, it is not easy to "fix" children's learning problems; but knowing the PASS characteristics is of immense value when educators try to assist young and old students to learn and solve problems effectively.

The procedures outlined in this chapter provide a number of options that enable school psychologists to assist teachers with students who have special learning needs. PBI and Planning Facilitation can be used in classrooms and in withdrawal (pullout) remedial settings. When there are opportunities for intervention on a small group basis, PREP can provide intensive reading remediation. Individualized instruction is appropriate in matching the child's characteristics to the PASS demands of the tasks. However, there is no "magic wand" solution to all the learning problems that teachers may confront in their classrooms. Nevertheless, use of the CAS along with a compatible instructional model can assist teachers in making changes to their repertoire of teaching practices and strategies and thereby increase children's learning.

TEST YOURSELF

1. Most academic tasks depend on

(a) Planning processes.

(b) Attention processes.

(c) Simultaneous processes.

(d) Successive processes.

(e) all the processes.

2. A PBI goal is different from instructions because it

(a) tells the child exactly what to do.

(b) makes the child decide what to do.

(c) encourages the child to think about how to complete the task.

(d) comes directly from the teacher.

3. If a child does not have a PASS weakness, the teacher should

(a) teach all the processes.

(b) teach the academic skill directly.

(c) consider other variables that may interfere with learning.

(d) all of the above.

(e) b and c only.

4. The essential difference between the Planning Facilitation method and PBI is that

(a) PBI involves direct instruction of strategies but facilitation does not.

(b) Planning Facilitation emphasizes teachers' plans.

(c) PBI is given in a group.

(d) Planning Facilitation is only given in small groups.

5. The PREP program is based on the assumption that failure in reading decoding is primarily due to a failure of

(a) Planning processes.

(b) Attention processes.

(c) Simultaneous processes.

(d) Successive processes.

(e) all the processes.

Answers: 1. e; 2. c; 3. e; 4. a; 5. d

References

Aiken, L. R. (1987). *Assessment of intellectual functioning.* Boston: Allyn & Bacon.

Albert, R. S., & Runco, M. A. (1986). The achievement of eminence: A model based on a longitudinal study of exceptionally gifted boys and their families. In R. J. Sternberg & J. E. Davidson (Eds.), *Conceptions of giftedness* (pp. 332–360). New York: Cambridge University Press.

Alexander, J., Carr, M., & Schwanenflugel, P. (1995). Development of metacognition in gifted children: Directions for future research. *Developmental Review, 15,* 1–37.

Amabile, T. M. (1983). Social psychology of creativity: A componential conceptualization. *Journal of Personality and Social Psychology, 45,* 357–377.

Amabile, T. M. (1996). *Creativity in context.* Boulder, CO: Westview Press.

American Psychiatric Association. (1987). *Diagnostic and statistical manual of mental disorders* (3rd ed. revised). Washington, DC: Author.

American Psychiatric Association. (1994). *Diagnostic and statistical manual of mental disorders* (4th ed.). Washington, DC: Author.

Anastasi, A., & Urbina, S. (1997). *Psychological testing.* Upper Saddle River, NJ: Prentice Hall.

Ashman, A. F., & Conway, R. N. F. (1989). *Cognitive strategies for special education.* London: Routledge.

Ashman, A. F., & Conway, R. N. F. (1993). *Using cognitive methods in the classroom.* New York: Routledge.

Ashman, A. F., & Conway, R. N. F. (1997). *An introduction to cognitive education: Theory and applications.* London: Routledge.

Ashman, A. F., & Das, J. P. (1980). Relation between planning and simultaneous-successive processing. *Perceptual and Motor Skills, 51,* 371–382.

Atkinson, L. (1991). Three standard errors of measurement and the Wechsler Memory Scale Revised. *Psychological Assessment, 3,* 136–138.

Barkley, R. A. (1990). *Attention Deficit Hyperactivity Disorder: A handbook for diagnosis and treatment.* New York: Guilford.

Barkley, R. A. (1994). Foreword in G. J. DuPaul & G. Stoner, *ADHD in the schools: Assessment and intervention strategies.* New York: Guilford.

Barron, F., & Harrington, D. (1981). Creativity, intelligence, and personality. *Annual Review of Psychology, 32,* 439–476.

Baxter, R., Cohen, S. B., & Ylvisaker, M. (1985). Comprehensive cognitive assessment. In M. Ylvisaker (Ed.), *Head injury rehabilitation: Children and adolescents* (pp. 247–274). San Diego, CA: College-Hill Press.

Begali, V. (1992). *Head injury in children and adolescents* (2nd ed.). Brandon, VT: Clinical Psychology Publishing.

Borkowski, J. G., & Peck, V. A. (1986). Causes and consequences of metamemory in gifted children. In R. J. Sternberg & J. E. Davidson (Eds.), *Conceptions of giftedness* (pp. 182–200). New York: Cambridge University Press.

Braden, J. P. (1997). The practical impact of intellectual assessment issues. *School Psychology Review, 26,* 242–248.

Brody, N. (1992). *Intelligence*. San Diego, CA: Academic Press.

Carlson J., & Das J. P. (1997). A process approach to remediating word-decoding deficiencies in chapter 1 children. *Learning Disability Quarterly, 20,* 93–102.

Carroll, J. B. (1995). [Review of the book *Assessment of cognitive processing: The PASS theory of intelligence*]. *Journal of Psychoeducational Assessment, 13,* 397–409.

Cohen, R. J., Swerdlik, M. E., & Phillips, S. M. (1992). *Psychological testing and assessment*. Mountain View, CA: Mayfield.

Cormier, P., Carlson, J. S., & Das, J. P. (1990). Planning ability and cognitive performance: The compensatory effects of a dynamic assessment approach. *Learning and Individual Differences, 2,* 437–449.

Crocker, L., & Algina, J. (1986). *Introduction to classical and modern test theory*. New York: Holt, Rinehart and Winston.

Cronbach, L. J. (1970). *Essentials of psychological testing* (3rd ed.). New York: Harper & Row.

Das, J. P. (1972). Patterns of cognitive ability in nonretarded and retarded children. *American Journal of Mental Deficiency, 77,* 6–12.

Das, J. P. (in press). *PASS Remedial Program*.

Das, J. P., Kar, B. C., & Parrila, R. K. (1996). *Cognitive planning: The psychological basis of intelligent behavior*. Thousand Oaks, CA: Sage Publications.

Das, J. P., & Kendrick, M. (1997). PASS Reading Enhancement Program: A short manual for teachers. *Journal of Cognitive Education, 5,* 193–208.

Das, J. P., Kirby, J. R., & Jarman, R. F. (1975). Simultaneous and successive syntheses: An alternative model for cognitive abilities. *Psychological Bulletin, 82,* 87–103.

Das, J. P., Kirby, J. R., & Jarman, R. F. (1979). *Simultaneous and successive cognitive processes*. New York: Academic Press.

Das, J. P., Mishra, R. K., & Pool, J. E. (1995). An experiment on cognitive remediation or word-reading difficulty. *Journal of Learning Disabilities, 28,* 66–79.

Das, J. P., & Naglieri, J. A. (1996). Mental retardation and assessment of cognitive processes. In J. W. Jacobson & J. A. Mulick (Eds.), *Manual of diagnosis and professional practice in mental retardation* (pp. 115–126). Washington, DC: American Psychological Association.

Das, J. P., Naglieri, J. A., & Kirby, J. R. (1994). *Assessment of cognitive processes*. Needham Heights, MA: Allyn & Bacon.

DuPaul, G. J., & Stoner, G. (1994). *ADHD in the schools: Assessment and intervention strategies*. New York: Guilford.

Elliott, C. D. (1990). *Differential Ability Scales: Introductory and technical handbook.* San Antonio, TX: The Psychological Corporation.

Esters, I. G., Ittenbach, R. F., & Han, K. (1997). Today's IQ tests: Are they really better than their historical predecessors? *School Psychology Review, 26,* 211–224.

Finke, R. A., Ward, T. B., & Smith, S. M. (1992). *Creative cognition.* Cambridge, MA: MIT Press.

Flanagan, D., Andrews, T., & Genshaft, J. (1997). The functional utility of intelligence tests with special education populations. In D. P. Flanagan, J. L. Genshaft, & P. L. Harrison (Eds.), *Contemporary intellectual assessment* (pp. 457–483). New York: Guilford.

Flavell, J. (1979). Metacognition and cognitive monitoring: A new area of cognitive-developmental inquiry. *American Psychologist, 34*(10), 906–911.

Getzels, J. W., & Jackson, P. W. (1962). *Creativity and intelligence: Explorations with gifted students.* New York: Wiley.

Gindis, B. (1996). [Review of the book *Assessment of cognitive processing: The PASS theory of intelligence*]. *School Psychology International, 17,* 305–308.

Goldberg, E. (1990). *Contemporary neuropsychology and the legacy of Luria.* Hillsdale, NJ: Erlbaum.

Green, G., Mackay, H. A., McIlvane, W. J., Saunders, R. R. & Sraci, S. (1990). Perspectives on relational learning in mental retardation. *American Journal of Mental Retardation, 95,* 249–259.

Grover, S. C. (1987). Level of planning skill as a predictor of variations in computer competency among intellectually gifted and non-gifted children. *Journal of Educational Research, 80*(3), 173–178.

Guastello, S. J., Shissler, J., Driscoll, J., & Hyde, T. (1998). Are some cognitive styles more creatively productive than others? *Journal of Creative Behavior, 32*(2), 77–91.

Gutentag, S., Naglieri, J. A., & Yeates, K. O. (1998). Performance of children with traumatic brain injury on the Cognitive Assessment System. *Assessment, 5,* 263–272.

Hammill, D. D., Leigh, J., McNutt, G., & Larsen, S. C. (1981). A new definition of learning disabilities. *Learning Disability Quarterly, 4,* 336–342.

Hay, I. (in press). Cognitive strategies in the secondary school. *Journal of Cognitive Education.*

Hynd, G. W., Voeller, K. K., Hern, K. L., & Marshall, R. M. (1991). Neurobiological basis of Attention-Deficit Hyperactivity Disorder (ADHD). *School Psychology Review, 20,* 174–186.

Idol, L. (1987). Group story mapping: A comprehension strategy for both skilled and unskilled readers. *Journal of Learning Disabilities, 20,* 196–205.

Jensen, A. R. (1980). *Bias in mental testing.* New York: Free Press.

Kar, B. C., Dash, U. N., Das, J. P., & Carlson, J. S. (1992). Two experiments on the dynamic assessment of planning. *Learning and Individual Differences, 5,* 13–29.

Kaufman, A. S. (1994). *Intelligent testing with the WISC-III.* New York: Wiley.

Kaufman, A. S., & Kaufman, N. L. (1983). *Kaufman Assessment Battery for Children.* Circle Pines, MN: American Guidance.

Kaufman, A. S., & Kaufman, N. L. (1993). *Kaufman Adolescent and Adult Intelligence Test.* Circle Pines, MN: American Guidance.

Kaufman A. S., & Kaufman, N. L. (1998). *Kaufman Test of Educational Achievement.* Circle Pines, MN: American Guidance.

Kavale, K. A., & Forness, S. R. (1984). A meta-analysis of the validity of the Wechsler Scale profiles and recategorizations: Patterns or parodies? *Learning Disability Quarterly, 7,* 136–151.

Kirby, J. R. (1984). *Cognitive strategies and educational performance.* New York: Academic Press.

Kirby, J. R., & Williams, N. H. (1991). *Learning problems: A cognitive approach.* Toronto: Kagan and Woo.

Kotarsky, D., & Mason, E. (in press). A review of the Cognitive Assessment System. *Insight.*

Lambert, N. L. (1990). Consideration of the Das-Naglieri Cognitive Assessment System. *Journal of Psychoeducational Assessment, 8,* 338–343.

Lehr, E. (1990). Incidence and etiology. In E. Lehr (Ed.), *Psychological management of traumatic brain injuries in children and adolescents* (pp. 1–14). Rockville, MD: Aspen Publishers.

Luria, A. R. (1966). *Human brain and psychological processes.* New York: Harper & Row.

Luria, A. R. (1973). *The working brain: An introduction to neuropsychology.* New York: Basic Books.

Luria, A. R. (1980). *Higher cortical functions in man* (2nd ed.). New York: Basic Books.

Luria, A. R. (1982). *Language and cognition.* New York: Wiley.

Luria, A. R., & Tsvetkova, L. S. (1990). *The neuropsychological analysis of problem solving* (A. Mikheyev & S. Mikheyev, Trans.). Orlando, FL: Paul M. Deutsch Press.

Mastropieri, M. A., & Schruggs, T. E. (1991). *Teaching students ways to remember.* Cambridge, MA: Brookline Books.

Matarazzo, J. (1972). *Wechsler's measurement and appraisal of adult intelligence* (5th ed.). Baltimore: Williams & Wilkins.

McCallum, R. S., & Karnes, F. A. (1987). The relationship between cognitive processing and intelligence among gifted students. *Educational and Psychological Research, 7*(3), 183–190.

McGrew, K. S., & Hessler, G. L. (1995). The relationship between the WJ-R Gf-Gc cognitive clusters and mathematics achievement across the life-span. *Journal of Psychoeducational Assessment, 13,* 21–38.

McGrew, K. S., Keith, T. Z., Flanagan, D. P., & Vanderwood, M. (1997). Beyond g: The impact of Gf-Gc specific cognitive abilities research on the future use and interpretation of intelligence tests in the schools. *School Psychology Review, 26,* 189–210.

McGrew, K. S., Werder, J. K., & Woodcock, R. W. (1991). *Woodcock-Johnson Technical Manual.* Itasca, IL: Riverside Publishing.

Miller, G., Galanter, E., & Pribram, K. (1960). *Plans and the structure of behavior.* New York: Henry Holt.

Mueller, H. H., Dennis, S. S., & Short, R. H. (1986). A meta-exploration of WISC-R factor score profiles as a function of diagnosis and intellectual level. *Canadian Journal of School Psychology, 2,* 21–43.

Naglieri, J. A. (1985). *Matrix Analogies Test, Expanded Form.* San Antonio, TX: The Psychological Corporation.

Naglieri, J. A. (1989). A cognitive processing theory for the measurement of intelligence. *Educational Psychologist, 24,* 185–206.

Naglieri, J. A. (1993). Pairwise and ipsative WISC-III IQ and Index Score comparisons. *Psychological Assessment, 5,* 113–116.

Naglieri, J. A. (1997a). Intelligence Knowns and Unknowns: Hits or Misses. *American Psychologist, 25,* 75–76.

Naglieri, J. A. (1997b). *Naglieri Nonverbal Ability Test.* San Antonio, TX: The Psychological Corporation.

Naglieri, J. A. (in press). How Valid Is the PASS Theory and CAS? *School Psychology Review.*

Naglieri, J. A., & Das, J. P. (1987). Construct and criterion related validity of planning, simultaneous, and successive cognitive processing tasks. *Journal of Psychoeducational Assessment, 5,* 353–363.

Naglieri, J. A., & Das, J. P. (1988). Planning-Arousal-Simultaneous-Successive (PASS): A Model for Assessment. *Journal of School Psychology, 26,* 35–48.

Naglieri, J. A., & Das, J. P. (1997a). *Cognitive Assessment System.* Itasca, IL: Riverside Publishing.

Naglieri, J. A., & Das, J. P. (1997b). *Cognitive Assessment System Administration and Scoring Manual.* Itasca, IL: Riverside Publishing.

Naglieri, J. A., & Das, J. P. (1997c). *Cognitive Assessment System Interpretive Handbook.* Itasca, IL: Riverside Publishing.

Naglieri, J. A., & Gottling, S. H. (1995). A cognitive education approach to math instruction for the learning disabled: An individual study. *Psychological Reports, 76,* 1343–1354.

Naglieri, J. A., & Gottling, S. H. (1997). Mathematics instruction and PASS cognitive processes: An intervention study. *Journal of Learning Disabilities, 30,* 513–520.

Naglieri, J. A., & Johnson, D. (in press). Improving Math Calculation Using a Cognitive Intervention Based on the PASS Theory. *Communiqué, 27.*

Pintner, R. (1923). *Intelligence testing.* New York: Henry Holt.

Pressley, M. P., & Woloshyn, V. (1995). *Cognitive strategy instruction that really improves children's academic performance* (2nd ed.). Cambridge, MA: Brookline Books.

Redmond, M. R., Mumford, M. D., & Teach, R. (1993). Putting creativity to work: Effects of leader behavior on subordinate creativity. *Organizational Behavior and Human Decision Processes, 55,* 120–151.

Reynolds, C. R. (1990). Conceptual and technical problems in learning disability diagnosis. In C. R. Reynolds & R. W. Kamphaus (Eds.), *Handbook of psychological & educational assessment of children: Intelligence & achievement* (pp. 571–592). New York: Guilford.

Robinson, A., & Clinkenbeard, P. R. (1998). Giftedness: An exceptionality examined. *Annual Review of Psychology, 48,* 117–139.

Roodin, P. A. (1996). Integrating cognitive theory, assessment and educational intervention. *Contemporary Psychology, 41,* 341–342.

Sattler, J. M. (1988). *Assessment of children* (3rd ed.). San Diego, CA: Author.

Savage, R. C., & Wolcott, G. F. (1994). Overview of acquired brain injury. In R. C. Savage & G. F. Wolcott (Eds.), *Educational dimensions of acquired brain injury* (pp. 3–12). Austin, TX: Pro-Ed.

Scheid, K. (1993). *Helping students become strategic learners.* Cambridge, MA: Brookline Books.

Schofield, N. J., & Ashman, A. F. (1987). The cognitive processing of gifted, high average, and low average ability students. *British Journal of Educational Psychology, 57*(1), 9–20.

Silverstein, A. B. (1993). Type I, Type II, and other types of errors in pattern analysis. *Psychological Assessment, 5,* 72–74.

Solso, R. L., & Hoffman, C. A. (1991). Influence of Soviet scholars. *American Psychologist, 46,* 251–253.

Sternberg, R. J., & Davidson, J. E. (Eds.). (1986). *Conceptions of giftedness.* New York: Cambridge University Press.

Swanson, H. L. (1991). *Handbook on the assessment of learning disabilities.* Austin, TX: Pro-Ed.

Telzrow, C. (1991). The school psychologist's perspective on testing students with traumatic head injury. *Journal of Head Trauma Rehabilitation, 6,* 23–26.

Thorndike, R. L., Hagen, E. P., & Sattler, J. M. (1986). *Stanford-Binet Intelligence Scale: Fourth edition.* Itasca, IL: Riverside Publishing.

U.S. Department of Education. (1997). *Individuals with Disabilities Education Act.* Washington, DC: U.S. Government Printing Office.

Wechsler, D. (1939). *Wechsler-Bellevue Intelligence Scale.* New York: The Psychological Corporation.

Wechsler, D. (1991). *Wechsler Intelligence Scale for Children, Third Edition, Manual.* San Antonio, TX: The Psychological Corporation.

Wechsler, D. (1992). *Wechsler Individual Achievement Test.* San Antonio, TX: The Psychological Corporation.

Wechsler, D. (1997). *Wechsler Adult Intelligence Scale, Third Edition.* San Antonio, TX: The Psychological Corporation.

Wilkinson, S. C. (1993). WISC-R profiles of children with superior intellectual ability. *Gifted Child Quarterly, 37*, 84–91.

Woodcock, R. W. (1998). *The WJ-R and Bateria-R in neuropsychological assessment: Research report number 1*. Itasca, IL: Riverside Publishing.

Woodcock, R. W., & Johnson, M. B. (1989a). *Woodcock-Johnson Revised Tests of Achievement: Standard and supplemental batteries*. Itasca, IL: Riverside Publishing.

Woodcock, R. W., & Johnson, M. B. (1989b). *Woodcock-Johnson Revised Tests of Cognitive Ability: Standard and supplemental batteries*. Itasca, IL: Riverside Publishing.

Yoakum, C. S., & Yerkes, R. M. (1920). *Army Mental Tests*. New York: Henry Holt.

Annotated Bibliography

This annotated bibliography summarizes important works relevant to the PASS theory and CAS. Entries are sequenced in order beginning with the early work by Miller and colleagues and Luria, moving to the initial work on Simultaneous and Successive processing, then to the work on PASS theory and eventually the CAS and related publications. This sequence provides a historical context of the development of work on the PASS theory and CAS.

1960s

Miller, G., Galanter, E., & Pribram, K. (1960). *Plans and the structure of behavior.* New York: Henry Holt.

This book is among the important works that encouraged psychologists to recognize the importance of cognition, and especially planning, as a uniquely human ability. Miller, Galanter, and Pribram's book helped psychologists move from the behavioral framework, with its exclusive focus on observable events, to a willingness to make inferences about cognitive processes. Moreover, the realization that behaviors could be interpreted as mental processes and that those processes could be the objects of psychological study formed the basis of the cognitive revolution. This book addresses important concepts such as the knowledge base for cognitive processing and planning as a way to control how operations are performed, both of which are integral to the PASS theory.

Luria, A. R. (1966). *Human brain and psychological processes.* New York: Harper & Row.

This book is a summary of approximately 25 years of research by Luria that details the neuropsychological syndromes of patients with brain damage. The text includes discussion of the functional relationships among brain regions and Luria's efforts to uncover the cerebral organization of mental activity. The book provides a historical review of work on the human brain and psychological processes and considers the role of the three functional units in activities such as voluntary movements, verbal thinking, and visual perception. Although it only touches on some of the important points more fully discussed in Higher Cortical Functions in Man *(1966, 1980), it uniquely details the important relationship between the brain and nonverbal behavior.*

Luria, A. R. (1966, 1980). *Higher cortical functions in man* (2nd ed. revised and expanded). New York: Basic Books.

Higher Cortical Functions in Man *is the most complete account of Luria's work in neuropsychology; it summarizes approximately 30 years of his efforts in understanding the relationships between cognition and the brain. In Luria's own words, in this book he "attempted to lay the foundation of neuropsychology as a new branch of science" (p. xxi). The 634-page book offers a discussion of major syndromes of the left cerebral hemisphere, detailed analysis of the frontal lobes, and considerable description of the tests used by Luria in his neuropsychological examinations. Interestingly, Tuber's introduction to the book includes a discussion about how standard tests of intelligence show little sensitivity to disturbances in cognitive functioning caused by brain injury, presumably because the tests are too psychometric. An alternative hypothesis put forth in this book is that standard tests fail because they do not measure those important cognitive processes included in Luria's three functional units (and measured by CAS). Nevertheless,* Higher Cortical Functions in Man *is an "important contribution to neuropsychological knowledge by one of the outstanding Soviet scientists of our time" (from Karl Pribram's preface, p. xvi).*

1970s

Das, J. P. (1972). Patterns of cognitive ability in nonretarded and retarded children. *American Journal of Mental Deficiency, 77,* 6–12.

This paper is especially noteworthy because it was the first time Das suggested that Luria's conceptualization of simultaneous and successive processes could be used to interpret results of a research study for persons with mental retardation. Das's study attempted to explain differences between nonretarded and retarded groups on the basis of Arthur Jensen's Level I and Level II distinction. The pattern of results did not fit expectations based on Level I and II. Instead, the pattern of performance for the groups was readily explainable by the simultaneous and successive processing interpretation of the tasks. Das suggests that measures of the two processes be developed and used to study the performance of exceptional children.

Luria, A. R. (1973). *The working brain: An introduction to neuropsychology.* New York: Basic Books.

In this 398-page book Luria presents in somewhat more abridged form his view of the working brain as a complex functional system described in Higher Cortical Functions of Man. *The first part of the book describes the concepts of functional organization and mental activity, including a discussion of the three functional units of attention; information processing (simultaneous and successive); and programming, regulation, and verification of activity (planning). The second part covers brain regions (e.g., the parietal regions and the organization of simultaneous syntheses). The third part addresses mental activities such as perception, movement, and memory. This book is an excellent introduction to Luria's approach to neuropsychology.*

Das, J. P., Kirby, J. R., & Jarman, R. F. (1979). *Simultaneous and successive cognitive processes*. New York: Academic Press.

This 247-page book is the first thorough discussion of how intelligence could be reconceptualized according to a theory of cognitive processing that arises from Luria's view of the three functional units (attention, simultaneous/successive, and planning). The authors emphasize that their theoretical approach is not to "tap as many abilities as possible, but to discover processes that might parsimoniously describe what was involved in those abilities [and] to conceptualize the basic cognitive functions" (p. xi). Although the book is titled Simultaneous and Successive Cognitive Processes, *the authors do not claim that these two processes constitute the entire scope of what should be measured. Although they recognize the importance of the three functional units, their work began with an examination of the second functional unit of simultaneous and successive processes (see annotation of Das, 1972). They describe what became the PASS theory, show how simultaneous and successive processes can be measured, summarize the relationships of these processes to achievement, identify the implications of this approach for understanding children with mental retardation and learning disabilities, and discuss the topic of intervention.*

1980s

Luria, A. R. (1982). *Language and Cognition*. New York: Wiley.

In the introduction to this book, James Wertsch reminds the reader of Macdonald Critchley's foreword to Luria's 1947 book Traumatic Aphasia, *writing "we cannot predict the fate of Luria's approach" (p. 13). From the view provided nearly 50 years later one can see that the work of Luria has evolved from theoretical analysis, to clinical practice, to a psychometrically formulated standardized instrument in the CAS. This translation from experimental to psychometric tests was positively regarded by Luria as noted in the foreword to Das, Naglieri, and Kirby (1994). There he communicated great satisfaction about the early work of Das in the development of Simultaneous and Successive tests. In fact, one of the most important influences during the development of the CAS was Luria's book* Language and Cognition *(1982). For example, it provided a critical basis for the development of CAS subtests such as Verbal-Spatial Relations, Sentence Repetition, and Sentence Questions. The 264-page book covers topics such as semantics, speech and the regulation of function, paradigmatic and syntagmatic aspects of language, speech, and the relationships between cerebral organization and pathological disruption of speech.*

Kirby, J. R. (1984). *Cognitive strategies and educational performance*. New York: Academic Press.

This book addresses a number of topics, including conceptualizations and studies of planning. The relationship between strategy use and planning is discussed, as is the importance of planning to educational performance and metacognition. The last two parts of the book describe cross-cultural studies and examinations of children with learning disabilities, attention deficits, and mental retardation. This book demonstrates the utility of several PASS experimental tests used in various countries.

Naglieri, J. A., & Das, J. P. (1987). Construct and criterion related validity of planning, simultaneous and successive cognitive processing tasks. *Journal of Psychoeducational Assessment, 5,* 353–363.

This paper was the first to report on the early experimental efforts to develop the CAS. The study involved a large sample of children who were administered tasks that eventually were adapted for inclusion in the published test. This paper demonstrates how Planning tests were as correlated with achievement as simultaneous and successive, thereby showing that the new measures had predictive value. The paper highlights possible advantages of measuring more than what is measured in traditional IQ tests.

Naglieri, J. A. (1989). A cognitive processing theory for the measurement of intelligence. *Educational Psychologist, 24,* 185–206.

This paper was the first to discuss the cognitive processing theory using the term PASS. The author stresses (a) the importance of measuring cognitive processes in contrast to the concept of IQ, and (b) the value of using a theory to identify the variables to be included. The PASS model was evaluated following from Dillon's proposed criteria; it was shown that the approach was a viable conceptualization of human abilities. It was concluded that the PASS model could provide the tools with which to make decisions about the cognitive processing status of children and adults that are relevant to diagnosis and have implications for intervention. The findings reported in Naglieri and Das (1997c) and in this text support those anticipated benefits.

1990s

Goldberg, E. (1990). *Contemporary neuropsychology and the legacy of Luria*. Hillsdale, NJ: Erlbaum.

Goldberg's 287-page edited book is a useful resource on the contributions Luria made to neuropsychology. It includes two summaries of Luria's work, one by Goldberg and one by Cole. The former outlines the distinctiveness of each of Luria's major contributions and places these events within the context of the evolving arena of neuropsychology. Also included are chapters on the frontal lobes and language, processes underlying memory impairments, hemispheric interaction, localization of processes, and historical discussion of several neuropsychological concepts. This book provides an excellent overview of the work of Luria, places it within a larger context of neuropsychology, and provides discussions of current thinking about various brain-behavior relationships.

Naglieri, J. A., & Das, J. P. (1990). Planning, Attention, Simultaneous and Successive (PASS) cognitive processes as a model for intelligence. *Journal of Psychoeducational Assessment, 8,* 303–337.

In early May 1990 the conference "Intelligence: Theories and Practice" took place in Memphis, Tennessee. Presentations were made by authors and representatives of major intelligence tests, including the yet-to-be-published CAS. In addition to the presentations, there were critiques of each approach and discussion of the importance of the various contributions. This paper is a summary of the presentation made by Naglieri at that conference and the reactions of some who critiqued the work. In her discussion of the PASS theory, N. L. Lambert suggests that the approach "could have potential for understanding failure in some aspects of classroom performance, as well as conditions of teaching and learning that need to be modified to improve school learning" (p. 342). Data subsequently presented supported these anticipated benefits. This paper establishes the PASS theory within the context of an alternative to traditional conceptualizations of IQ and demonstrates that the method offers important advantages.

Kirby, J. R., & Williams, N. H. (1991). *Learning problems: A cognitive approach.* Toronto: Kagan and Woo.

This book provides an example of how the PASS theory can be used to conceptualize the learning problems of children. Kirby and Williams use the PASS theory as a superstructure by which to understand academic failure and provide a discussion of the cognitive processing components of a number of school activities. For example, they discuss the PASS processing components involved in spelling, arithmetic, and reading and provide four chapters (each corresponding to a PASS process) for diagnosis and remediation of learning problems. This 273-page book is a valuable resource for practitioners who use the CAS for diagnosis and remediation of children's academic problems.

Das, J. P., Naglieri, J. A., & Kirby, J. R. (1994). *Assessment of cognitive processes.* Needham Heights, MA: Allyn & Bacon.

This book is based on the idea that "progress in the field of human intellectual assessment cannot be achieved if 'improvements' consist mainly of revisions of old tests or reconceptualizations of the tasks included in old measures" (p. 12). Part I discusses the restructuring of intelligence according to a cognitive processing perspective, and in particular the PASS theory. Part II discusses the PASS processes and tests that have been developed to measure them. Part III provides a closer look at the tests included in the PASS theory and summaries of published research involving various topics. Part IV is devoted to analyzing PASS profiles for exceptional children and moving from assessment to remediation. It concludes with a philosophical discussion of the work within the greater context of the field and promotes the view that *"we are on the edge of a major transition from old theories that limited us to new approaches that offer alternatives"* (p. 204). *This 236-page book summarizes the literature for the period between the publication of Das, Kirby, and Jarman (1979) and 1994.*

Das, J. P., Kar, B. C., & Parrila, R. K. (1996). *Cognitive planning: The psychological basis of intelligent behavior.* Thousand Oaks, CA: Sage Publications.

This 202-page book provides a primarily theoretical discussion of planning. It begins with a review of literature on planning from a historical, cognitive, neuropsychological, and developmental perspective. This section includes a discussion of the PASS theory, in which planning plays an important role. The second part contains summaries of empirical studies on various aspects of planning in a variety of situations. The book is a useful theoretical discussion of planning as it relates to intelligence, strategy use, metacognition, and problem solving.

Ashman, A. F., & Conway, R. N. F. (1997). *An introduction to cognitive education: Theory and applications.* New York: Routledge.

The cognitive revolution described by Miller, Galanter, and Pribram (1960) and the neuropsychological work of Luria (1966, 1970) formed the foundation for the cognitive approach to education described in this 268-page book. Ashman and Conway show how cognitive theory and principles of assessment, instruction, remediation, and clinical practice can be applied to the field of education. This approach, called cognitive education, is presented as a method to guide instruction and to assist psychologists when making the connection between a child's cognitive processing status and instruction. The book is divided into three sections: an introduction to cognitive education, ways of assessing intellectual skills (e.g., K-ABC and CAS), and instruction and remediation (e.g., PREP and Planning Facilitation).

Naglieri, J. A., & Das, J. P. (1997). *Cognitive Assessment System Interpretive Handbook.* Itasca, IL: Riverside Publishing.

This book summarizes the literature on CAS and PASS theory covering advancements from the publication of Das, Naglieri, and Kirby (1994) until publication of the test in 1994. Most important, the book presents evidence for the PASS theory as operationalized by the CAS, including the most comprehensive and inclusive study of the theory. The book's inclusion of research on the theory involving approximately 3,000 normal and exceptional children makes it a good resource for researchers and practitioners as well. Methods for interpretation of the CAS and extension of the PASS results to intervention were first articulated in Das et al. (1994) and are expanded in this volume. Of all the works on PASS, this one presents the most empirical evidence.

Naglieri, J. A., & Gottling, S. H. (1997). Mathematics instruction and PASS cognitive processes: An intervention study. *Journal of Learning Disabilities, 30,* 513–520.

For many years, researchers have attempted to show that IQ test results are relevant to instructional planning. This paper illustrates that the PASS processes do show important relationships to intervention and can be used in the selection of instructional methods. The study showed that children with learning disabilities differentially benefited from an instruction that encouraged them to better utilize planning processes when completing math computation worksheets containing problems taken directly from the curriculum. This study, like Naglieri and Gottling (1995) and previous published papers, illustrates the importance of knowing a child's PASS profile when making instructional decisions.

Gutentag, S., Naglieri, J. A., & Yeates, K. O. (1998). Performance of children with traumatic brain injury on the Cognitive Assessment System. *Assessment, 5,* 263–272.

This is the first study to be published specifically on results from a study of the CAS. The investigation showed that the test is sensitive to the cognitive deficits evidenced by children who experienced traumatic brain injury. These deficits in planning and attention, formerly not detectable with traditional tests, offer important insights into the problems experienced by these children. The authors suggest that the CAS can be useful when working with this type of child.

Index

About the Author

Jack A. Naglieri is Professor of School Psychology and Psychology at Ohio State University where he has taught since 1982. He also holds appointments as a Senior Researcher at Ohio State University's Nisonger Center and the Devereux Foundation's Institute for Clinical Training and Research. He obtained his Bachelor's degree in Psychology from Long Island University, Master of Science from St. John's University, and Ph.D. in Educational Psychology from the University of Georgia in 1979. The author of more than 125 scholarly papers and chapters in psychological journals, he has focused his efforts on reconceptualizing intelligence since the late 1970s. He is a Fellow of APA Division 16, holds a Diplomate in Assessment Psychology from the American Board of Assessment Psychology, and is a licensed Psychologist and certified as a School Psychologist in several states. He is a coauthor of *Assessment of Cognitive Processes: The PASS Theory of Intelligence* (Das, Naglieri, & Kirby, 1994). Naglieri is also the author of the *Das-Naglieri Cognitive Assessment System* (Naglieri, Das, 1997), *Devereux Scales of Mental Disorders* (Naglieri, LeBuffe, & Pfeiffer, 1994), *Devereux Behavior Rating Scale-School Form* (Naglieri, LeBuffe, & Pfeiffer, 1993), *Draw A Person: Screening Procedure for Emotional Disturbance* (Naglieri, McNeish, & Bardos, 1990), and *Draw A Person: Quantitative Scoring System* (Naglieri, 1988).